Bruce Tulloh was Britain's most successful distance runner of the 1960s, winning a national title or setting a national record every year from 1957 until his retirement from amateur competition in 1967. He represented Britain and England at all distances from 1,500 metres to 10,000 metres on the track, as well as in road and cross-country races, and competed in Olympic, European and Commonwealth Games.

He won a gold medal in the 5,000 metres in the 1962 European Games, and for many years held the British and European records for two miles, three miles and six miles. In 1969 he set a record for the America Transcontinental run from Los Angeles to New York.

As Secretary of the International Athletics Club he helped to organize coaching courses for British team members from 1964 to 1967. Since 1965 he has been teaching biology and coaching athletes at school and college level. Between 1971 and 1973 he taught at Kenyatta College, Nairobi, where he ran a coaching course for the Kenya team prior to the 1972 Olympics. Since 1973 he has been in charge of athletics and cross-country at Marlborough College and has recently spent a year at Kent School in Connecticut.

Bruce Tulloh is a Contributing Editor of *Running* magazine.

By the same author

Long Distance Running (with M. Hyman)
Tulloh on Running
Four Million Footsteps
World Athletics Handbook 1970
The Olympic Games
Naturally Fit
Natural Fitness
Modern Orienteering Training (with W. Holloway)
The Complete Jogger
Biosocial Aspects of Sport (ed)
The Marathon Book (with A. Etchells and N. Wilson)

BRUCE TULLOH

The Complete Distance Runner

PANTHER
Granada Publishing

Panther Books
Granada Publishing Ltd
8 Grafton Street, London W1X 3LA

Published by Panther Books 1983

ISBN 0-586-05976-8

Printed and bound in Great Britain by
Cox & Wyman Ltd, Reading
Set in Times

Contents

List of Training Schedules and Tables

Schedules

Tables

Acknowledgements

Brendan Foster's training schedules first appeared in his autobiography *Brendan Foster*, published by William Heinemann Ltd (1978).

Some of the schedules in Chapter 7 and part of Chapter 11 have previously appeared in *Running* magazine. The training schedules for Joyce Smith and Christine Benning were taken from *Athletics Weekly*. My thanks are due to Heinemann and to the editors of those magazines for permission to use this material, and to Nick Brawn for providing the majority of the photographs.

Somewhere there is a runner who is training alone. No one notices when he sets personal bests, but he keeps running on. This book is dedicated to him.

Foreword

Fifteen years ago I wrote a book called *Tulloh on Running*. It was the distillation of twenty years of competition, ten of them as a British international. At that time I thought that I really knew all there was to know about running. I had raced internationally at every distance from 800m to 20 miles, track, road and cross-country.

Fifteen years later I know more, but I realize how much more we still have to learn about this apparently simple sport. When I ran from Los Angeles to New York I realized that neither the physiologists nor the athletes really knew much about the problems of running very long distances. I was lucky to be able to get sound practical advice from one of the few men left in the world who had done the journey before, the late Pete Gavuzzi, hero of the 1929 Transcontinental Race. I appreciated the value of having advice from someone who had been through it all and knew just what was involved.

I thought I knew a lot about the limits of human endurance, but now, having spent time with the Tarahumara Indians of Mexico and the pastoral nomads of East Africa, I know that the true limits are beyond those which 'civilized' man has set for himself.

I thought I knew quite a lot about running shoes, their advantages and disadvantages, at least enough to know that most of the time I was better off running in bare feet. Now I see that we are beginning to solve the problems of adapting the human foot to running on the man-made road, but we still have a way to go.

Above all, I felt I knew a lot about human motivation,

what makes one man a winner and another a loser. I had analysed my own motives very closely and I had produced successful teams. Now there are ten, twenty or a hundred times more runners in the world than there were twenty years ago, comprising men and women of all ages, nationalities and occupations. They have many different reasons for running and as many ways of achieving victory, few of which involve being first over the line. Perhaps there are as many ways of achieving satisfaction in running as in life.

When I started running we relied mostly on the oral tradition of the running clubs. Today's new wave of runners are not part of the running tradition; most of them have to get their knowledge by making their own mistakes. In my last thirty-five years of running I have seen most of the mistakes that can be made, and made most of them myself. Now that I am coaching scores of athletes a year instead of just one, I realize that one system will not suit everybody. Having coached athletes in different parts of the world I appreciate how much the basic assumptions of the runner condition his image of himself and his visions of the future.

My excuse for writing a totally new book is that I find that newcomers to the sport are asking the same questions over and over again, and their view of the running world and its scope is limited by their own narrow experience. It is my hope that they will find some of the answers in these pages – though I hope it won't stop them looking further – and benefit from my own experience.

Bruce Tulloh
Marlborough, August 1983

1
The Essence of Running

Lord Byron once told a friend that he had known only three truly happy hours during his whole existence. Such noble melancholy is not for me. The seventeenth-century Chinese writer Chin Shengt'an, trapped indoors in rainy weather, made a list of recurrent happy moments; he reached thirty-three before the rain stopped! None was particularly elevated, some were purely sensuous: 'To cut with a sharp knife a bright green water-melon on a big scarlet plate on a summer afternoon. Is this not happiness?'

Running is like that for me. It is a direct entry into a world of sensuous experience, something which I myself feel, not filtered through a television screen or passed on second hand through a book. Not all the experiences are good ones, but as I get older I get better at avoiding the bad ones. Sometimes I get frightened, sometimes irritable, sometimes exhilarated, but all the time I know that I am 100 per cent alive. In some cases the intensity of the experience has burned it into my brain, so that I only have to pick up an old programme to have a total recall of time past, remembering the kind of person I was twenty years ago, how the race went and what we did afterwards. More often the memories drift up like leaves and have to be sifted through in the pages of my diary. An article by David Sutton in *Running* magazine (April 1983) expressed this with beauty and economy:

> I would rather lose most things I own than those pages of my past. The knowledge that one gets from running is of a kind becoming rare in our world. It is primary knowledge. You run ten miles and you find out something – about rain, or moonlight or

gutsache or yourself, and it's yours. No one gave it to you and no one can take it away. It's there in the mind always, like a circle of lamplight on a dark night.

I am a competitive animal, there is no denying it, and for me racing is the real thing. Experience is sharper, the highs are higher and the depths more abysmal than at any other time. After the perfect race I sleep well and wake up happy. Let me describe one to you. It wasn't a big occasion, and I was no longer in my first flush of youth – perhaps for that reason it was a rare encounter with perfection.

The race was in the autumn, when I have more time for training. It was quite near home, and it was 5 miles. Since I no longer have either the disposition or the speed for a real burn-up over a mile, and am too lazy to put in more than 30 miles a week, except under extreme provocation, it was just the right distance. There was a veteran's prize, for which I stood a good chance, and I felt that I should finish pretty well up. There was a bigger race on 50 miles away, so the real stars would probably not bother with our small-town 5-miler. Deep down inside, the little serpent, Ambition, whispered 'you might even win this one'. Being a mature and balanced person I decided that the object was to prove fitness and to ward off the inevitable decline. Five minutes 15 seconds per mile would be a good target, that would total just over 26 minutes.

As the race was not far from home, I was able to train over the course. It had a couple of hills, but the last three-quarters of a mile was mostly downhill, flattening out at the finish. It was a good autumn day, high clouds, a slightly chilly breeze to tickle the bare shoulders; I don't like wearing T-shirts, they make me feel constricted. I warmed up over the last part of the course with some of my boys, working off my own worries by telling them how to pace themselves. I had arrived in plenty of time to get my number, go through my warm-up routine and perform all the pre-race activities which pre-race nerves generate. The number of competitors increased steadily; there must have been 200, and many of them looked like real runners, with good track suits and classy racing shoes. They too went through their stretching routines in a professional way.

They pushed us back on to the start line, in a rather congested stony lane. I kept my sweat shirt on until the last minute, moving about while the start was held up for late comers, and then I managed to infiltrate myself in to the front group, but not on the start line, as I didn't want to have to sprint away. In the old days people were much more aggressive about lining up, but with the 'new wave' they seem content to grade themselves by ability – except for the teenage boys. There were several of these in front of me, eager for early glory and a picture in the local rag.

When the gun went, the boys sprinted away, leaving just enough space for me to get going immediately. The track was stony and narrow, and a runner coming in from the side checked the boy in front of me. He stumbled, leaned forwards and, as if in slow motion, I could see him trying to stay upright for a couple of strides until he overbalanced and went down. That was long enough for me to veer round him, increasing my pace slightly to avoid being trampled by the crowd I knew was right behind me. I allowed my pace to drop slightly, so that others came past me and I was able to relax behind them. The near upset had startled me, so I had to minimize the disturbance.

Out on to proper road, and somebody came past quite fast and took the lead. I scrutinized him; he wasn't anyone very good, so I stayed with the bunch behind. The pace seemed fast enough, and as we came to the first mile marker my watch read 5 minutes 8 seconds. The mile markers always cause a surge of pace by those who have ambitious schedules, and somebody else took up the running in a determined fashion. Two members of the group went after him, and I followed them, trying to close the gap gradually. We came to the first short incline and the leaders slowed down. I adjusted my stride to the hill, and checked that I was not wasting energy from any unnecessary tension in my arms or shoulders. Keeping my stride short and smooth, I found that I was moving up on the leading man. As we came over the top of the hill we had broken clear. I let him lead down the next bit, and we came past 2 miles in 10 minutes 21 seconds. Now we started a steady climb, which went on for 1½ miles. At the end of this stretch was a long downhill run, which would take us past the 4-mile mark. There was no one around on the uphill drag, just the two of us. I knew he was quite good, but he was only twenty-one, so perhaps he lacked mental toughness. We would soon find out.

I put my head down and increased the pace, thinking of keeping the pressure on. He came with me up the first rise, and then I tried again. It was beginning to hurt me, so he should be feeling it too. Sure enough, his steps sounded more distant. Now I had a gap open, it was time to increase it while my opponent was mentally weak. I looked at the road ahead, and picked the most direct line around the curves, urging myself to keep up the rhythm, trying to relax my shoulders and yet maintain my arm action up the hill. Times didn't matter now, I had a chance of winning this. We came into the stretch through the pine wood. I love running through pines; it reminds me of Finland. The last bit of hill was in sight now – treat it as a winning post. Over the top of the hill I changed into a long, floating stride, so that I would be going fast down the hill while he was still plodding up to it. Experience told me that though I felt pretty tired when I reached the top, I would recover on the way down, so I got moving without waiting to recover.

Only a mile to go, and I couldn't hear the man behind me. That meant he must be 10 or 15 seconds down. So as long as I didn't crack up I was going to win. A bend in the road meant that I could afford the quick glance back I had been denying myself during the pressure period. I had 70 yards at least and he didn't look threatening. Just keep it going now, keep the stride long and don't slow down, even though I can feel my stomach muscles cramping up. Think of winning, think of my daughters waiting at the finish. This is for you, twins. Now there are only 600 yards to go. I should try to increase the pace again, in case the man behind gets crazy ideas about winning. Now I'm getting into the crowd near the finish, I can afford to smile and wave. Round the corner and there is the finish; I dash in the last 30 yards, and the clock reads 25 minutes 58 seconds. That's grand. Maybe I could run a lot faster when I was young, but that time makes me feel very good. Now for a shower and a beer and a really good meal. I don't have to prove myself for a long time now.

All right, it's a selfish pleasure, and what about all the people who finished after me? Were they only there to gratify the egotism of the winner? No, because there is something to be gained by everybody in running. We are all seeking for excellence, or at least for improvement. Doing well in a race is the pinnacle, but all the steps in the upward climb are worthwhile. I must have been to over thirty races in that year, and that was the only one I won, and only because the opposition happened to be weak. I had had some seconds and thirds and fourths, and they all gave me a lot of pleasure. I came sixty-seventh in a marathon race, but set a personal best and got a small prize, so that gave me satisfaction too, in spite of the deep exhaustion. In another marathon I ran deliberately slowly, so that, although the final time was not impressive, I had a lot of fun roaring through the field for the last few miles, and finishing fresh and strong.

All this was building up to the Boston Marathon, which

was almost a total disaster. In spite of all my experience and careful pace judgement, I suffered a muscle pull at 10 miles. It might have been the unusually warm weather, or it might have been lack of preparation for the notoriously fast downhill stretches, or it might just have been my ageing legs. I managed to stay more or less on schedule to the half distance, which I went through in just under 1 hour 15 minutes, but from then on my legs became more and more painful. Encouraged by Clive, my son, who kept passing me water and sponging my legs, I struggled painfully up Heartbreak Hill and down to the finish. For the next three days I could hardly walk, let alone jog. Could this really be justified? Wasn't it ridiculous for a middle-aged man, well past his prime, trying to match men twenty years younger?

This is a question which must be answered, and this is my excuse for indulging in so much personal detail. First, the experience is valid at any age. Our quest for self-knowledge or self-perfection should not stop at thirty, or fifty, or at any time. Second, the enterprise is worth doing just *because* success is not guaranteed. When we start, we know that there is the possibility of failure, so when we do fail we have to be philosophical about it, and learn from it. A man who has not learned to accept that he may fail is not human. A man's greatness is measured by his ability to rise above his failures.

This brings us back to the essence of running, which is self-mastery. I can think of no other sport in which this is more true. It is true of mountain-climbing and surfing, but these are less accessible to the ordinary man or woman. In running we can each find our own mountain and climb it in our own way. The occasional writer or poet can find the right words to express it but, for most of us, if we start to voice our feelings about running, it just sounds banal. So we don't talk about it, we just run.

Running is like dancing. It is a pure expression of the individual through the medium of his or her own body. We cannot all be poets or dancers, but given good health we can all run. By running we can gain this feeling of being in control of our own bodies and our own lives, and by running we can express ourselves in relation to the world around us. The runner knows what the world is like when he feels the wind in his face. No one has expressed this aspect better than the running poet, Charles Hamilton Sorley; although he died in the First World War at the age of twenty, he wrote a few lines which are deservedly immortal:

> We swing ungirded hips
> and lightened are our eyes,
> The rain is on our lips,
> we do not run for prize.
> We know not whom we trust,
> nor whitherward we fare,
> but we run because we must
> Through the great wide air.
>
> Does the tearing tempest pause?
> Do the tree-tops ask it why?
> So we run without a cause,
> 'Neath the big bare sky.
>
> ('Song of the Ungirt Runner')

The same sort of feelings are expressed by Walt Whitman in his 'Song of the Open Road':

> Afoot and light-hearted, I take to the open road,
> Healthy, free, the world before me,
> The long brown path before me, leading wherever I choose.

So, running is freedom, it is expression, it is a pouring out of the life-force within us. What surprises and gratifies me is that it is also a means of bringing people together.

If you meet a group of marathon runners the night before the race, you would say that, with a few exceptions, they are a pretty unsociable bunch. Runners are often loners, and before races they become more introverted than usual. Come the morning of the race, however, you will see things starting to change. The euphoria of peak physical condition, with a touch of nervousness, start strangers talking to one another. When the race gets going they discover people around them who are going for the same time. They discover that they have more in common with these strangers than they have with many people they have known all their lives.

A friend of mine got into the London Marathon, the first race of any kind he had ever run in. He wanted to stop smoking and feel younger. What he didn't realize until the race got started was that he really wanted to be part of a crowd of idealists, striving together for a common cause. He found himself running at the same pace as a young American. After a mile or two they got talking. After a few more miles they exchanged names and passed drinks to each other. When one hit a bad patch, the other helped him through. They ran together for the entire race, until they got within 300 yards of the finish, when they were split up in the throng of runners and failed to find each other after finishing. All my friend knew of the American was his first name and the fact that he was at an air base near Oxford. He kept ringing people until he tracked down his running companion, and they had a celebration dinner together, celebrating their joint success and their common humanity. What was their time? Does it matter?

The best thing that has emerged from the running boom has been this feeling of common humanity that comes out of shared experience. It is common knowledge that desperate situations, such as war, bring out the best in men and women alike, and philosophers have lamented that this sense of comradeship does not survive the balmy days of peace. Demagogues have succeeded in creating the mood artificially, by uniting a people against a common enemy, but little good has ever come out of that. The continued growth of the running movement in the western world resembles nothing so much as a religious movement. It has its active evangelists, its hordes of converts eagerly spreading the word, and that general diffusion of good-will that embraces a host of other well-meaning organizations and charities, from the British Heart Foundation to the followers of Sri Chin Moy.

How can such a simple activity as running mean so many things to so many people? It arouses fierce national rivalry at Olympic level. To eastern European countries, particularly East Germany and the Soviet Union, sport is a field in the ideological battle. State money, organization, medical and educational resources are used lavishly to produce and support winning national teams. The victories of those teams are held up as proof of the superiority of the communist system, regardless of the methods by which those victories were won.

We may sneer at the 'win at all costs' philosophy in this guise, but how many of us unconsciously subscribe to it in other forms? Are we right to hail the winner of the Olympic Decathlon or the New York Marathon just because he wins, without considering the cost of winning? Is it right that the winner of a major race should pick up $20,000 when youngsters from a back-street club are having to pay $5 a head to enter the race? Is it right to subsidize the successful runner, or to give him a scholarship to a college because of his ability?

Perhaps the most puzzling question is this: how is it that a sport which, on the face of it, is as directly competitive as fighting, should be a means of bringing people together?

How can it meet the emotional needs of the sixteen-year-old boy, the middle-aged housewife and the retired doctor? Although I can only guess at some of the answers, I hope that I can clarify matters by considering, in the next chapter, the roles that running has played in our society up to the present time.

2
The Development of Running

Man has always run. Apart from his brain, the chief thing that distinguishes him from the anthropoid ape is the lower limb development. The ape's feet are not specialized for walking, as our feet are. Their legs are more flexible, but not so efficient for running. The human, like the horse, has limited flexibility at the knee and ankle joints, but this limitation ensures that when we use our leg muscles, we move in a straight line.

It may well be that man as a runner reached his peak in prehistoric times and that our present efforts are feeble attempts to regain our former excellence. In countries where it is still the rule to travel on foot, 20 miles is an easy journey and 50 miles is a long day. We Europeans have forgotten what it was like to use our own legs. In our written tradition the horse predominates. Perhaps the worn ridgeways could tell us the story, but there is no way of knowing because the oral tradition died long ago.

In America, where the horse is a recent introduction, legends of Indian running still remain, and have been written down. There is a great tradition of running in Indian tribal lore. Not only were the young men trained to be hardy for hunting and fighting, but there were traditional brotherhoods of runners, message carriers, who could run all day. The schedules of modern distance runners would be child's play to these men, for whom a 100-mile run across open country was just a day's work. I can say this with confidence, because there still remains one nation of Indians which has kept its running tradition through to the present day. These are the Tarahumaras.

If you take a plane to El Paso and a bus to Chihuahua, you can take a train on the Chihuahua al Pacifico railroad, which runs through the Sierra Madre Occidentale. If you get off in the mountains at Creel, and find a truck going in the right direction, you come to Sisoguichic, in the heart of the Tarahumara country. These people, a branch of the Apache nation, came into these mountains over 1000 years ago. As the Mexicans moved into the fertile land, the Tarahumaras moved further into the hills, keeping their own language and their own way of life, in which running forms a central part. More than anything else, to be a great runner is to be a hero.

In the summer of 1971 I spent a few weeks in their country, to find out if the legends about their running were true. I witnessed one of their races – not a big one, but a fairly routine fixture, approximately 120 miles over rough roads, at an altitude of 6000 feet. The races do not involve straightforward running. They are relay races, with four to six runners in each team. The first man flicks a light wooden ball forwards with his toes to the man in front, who passes it on ahead, while the first man runs to the front of the line. This is not merely more interesting than straight running, but requires more skill and effort. The big races, which have been witnessed by outside observers, last for forty-eight hours, in which over 160 miles are covered. All the runners must stay in the race, and as they run laps up and down the mountain valleys they are given food and drink by their supporters, who, having bet heavily on the result, will do anything to keep them going.

The Tarahumaras are not very fast, so far as we can tell, because they do not run short distances like 10,000m or marathons, but their stamina sets an example which the rest of the running world has yet to follow. It is said that when they were asked if they would send runners to represent Mexico in the 1932 (Los Angeles) Olympics, they asked what the distance was. Told that it was 26 miles, they suggested sending some of their women! The main race for Tarahumara women is 60 miles.

Such are our origins, though we have come a long way from them. When man was a hunter, and even when he was a pastoral nomad, the ability to run was highly prized, but when he settled down to planting crops and living in towns, running became an occupation for specialists only. In all the ancient civilizations for which we have records we hear of running messengers. Before the invention of clocks and watches there was no method of timing their performances except by the sun, and so we have nothing really accurate, particularly as the measurement of distance was not standardized. Probably the most reliable source comes from the ancient Greeks, which is why we have the legend of Pheidippides. It is unlikely that he ran from Marathon to Athens after the battle of Marathon, because the event was not reported by contemporary historians, or by anyone until 400 years later, but he did run from Athens to Sparta, a distance of about 136 miles, which is rather more impressive. We can think ourselves lucky that this distance has not become the fashionable one to race over!

The messengers, or footmen, carried on the tradition of man the runner, and their performances merely serve to underline the great powers of endurance which human beings can show when they have to. The nature of the human frame and human physiology cannot be any different now – genes are unlikely to have altered in the ninety generations which separate us from the Ancient Greeks. The performances which have come down from ancient times, though impressive bearing in mind the bad roads of those days, are not unbeatable. There is a report of a Persian footman in the Ottoman Empire running from Constantinople to Adrianople, about 125 miles, in under 24 hours in the fifteenth century, and in 1548 an Irish footman named Langham ran 148 miles in under 42 hours.

Inevitably, the next step from running for a living was to run for a wager or a prize. In Britain, this change seems to have occurred in the eighteenth century, by which time distances could be accurately measured and timed. It was a significant change. Before it occurred, runners were merely another form of servant, now they became special people, professional sportsmen, entertainers perhaps. Their performances came to be measures of prowess, which led others to try to emulate them.

In these early days there was no distinction between 'professional' and 'amateur', perhaps because the gulf between the 'haves' and 'have-nots' was too obvious to need defining. When gentlemen of the upper classes pitted themselves against professional runners they were doing it just for the love of sport, though a profound observer might have found psychological reasons for their need to prove themselves. The most famous of the 'gentleman athletes' was Captain Barclay Allardyce, who walked 1000 miles in 1000 hours in 1799. He walked a mile in each hour, a feat of extraordinary patience. Although not a runner, his time of 19 hours for a 100-mile walk, in 1806, is still impressive today.

Barclay Allardyce was a Regency man. The development of separate amateur and professional sports took place in early Victorian times, and there are surely many PhDs to be mined from this particular seam. We had the Industrial Revolution, cities springing up and the countryside emptying, we had great poverty and great wealth, the resurgence of religion as a dominant force in society, and the creation of new classes. No doubt it was the dangerous fluidity of Victorian society which led to the formation of such rigid rules of conduct – the books of etiquette were written in this era and so were the rules of sport.

In the nineteenth century, running, like football and

boxing, went in two directions. It flourished as a professional spectator sport, drawing huge crowds and attracting big gambling interests, and it developed as a worthy occupation for the amateur athlete and the young gentlemen of the public schools of Britain. For many years the incentive of cash produced far greater running performances than the pursuit of fitness. Because the professional events demanded spectators, most races were held in enclosed arenas, initially on grass tracks. The longest distances run were normally 10 miles or one-hour races and they were usually run as challenge matches between two men, although a champion might challenge all comers and run against four or five individuals. The performances of some of the mid-nineteenth-century champions were excellent. As far back as 1852, the English professional William Howitt ran 11 miles in 59 minutes 20 seconds. In the 1860s there was a tremendous upsurge of public interest in distance running when the American Indian Louis Bennett, who ran under the name of Deerfoot, started touring Britain and throwing out challenges to the best British runners. This in itself is evidence for the existence of a high standard of professional running in the USA at that time, because Bennett thought that he would win more races, as well as making more impact, in Britain than in America. In his first season, 1861, he defeated most of his opponents over a variety of distances, but, as always happens, his performances led to an all-round rise in standards, and he had to fight hard to maintain his supremacy in the next two seasons. In doing so, he set world best times for 10 miles and the hour, and, more important, set new standards in racing tactics. In a word, the image of distance running was enhanced. Throughout the 1850s and 1860s new athletic clubs were formed in Britain, athletic tracks were laid down and more and more of the public schools included running in their sports programmes. In the winter months the sport of 'hares and hounds', based on the hunting tradition which was common throughout the country, was a good way of exercising the boys in boarding schools. The first known school cross-country run is the Crick Run, at Rugby, which goes back to 1837. The first cross-country running club, Thames Hare and Hounds, was formed in 1867.

Both the amateur and the professional sides of running continued to grow. The most remarkable feats of endurance so far seen were performed by the professional runners who took part in the six-day races in the 1870s and 1880s. The man who originated this, the American walker, Edward Weston, became the first man to cover 500 miles in six days, in 1874. Such was the incentive of the huge money prizes, accompanied by vast public interest – and a lot of betting – that by 1888 the record had been improved to 623 miles, by the British runner George Littlewood. These races were performed on small indoor tracks, usually ten or eleven laps to the mile, which makes them even more remarkable. The record for 24 hours, just over 150 miles, set in 1882 by Charlie Rowell, has been beaten by only a handful of people in the subsequent 100 years.

Most of us think of modern running as originating with the first modern Olympic Games, in 1896, but in fact those games were the apex of a pyramid which had been growing for fifty years. Although the Marathon to Athens race of 1896 was the first to bear that name, long distance races, as we have seen, were being put on long before that time. The oldest long distance road race to have been held regularly is the Around the Bay race in Hamilton, Ontario, which was inaugurated in 1894. The special quality of the long distance runner must have been in the mind of Michel Bréal, the French professor who put forward the idea of including 'the marathon race' in the revival of the ancient Olympic Games. He knew that the legendary run of

Pheidippides the messenger was a potent symbol of Greek freedom, and he proposed to his friend Baron Pierre de Coubertin that a race starting on the site of the battle, the plain of Marathon, and finishing in the new stadium, would appeal to the popular imagination. One wonders what would have happened if Marathon had been 10 miles from Athens, or 50 miles. Would the distance still have the same magic? We shall never know, because from 1896 onwards this distance of approximately 40km became the accepted test of the long distance man. The first wave of 'marathon fever' swept over America, or at least the east coast, when the first Boston Marathon was held in 1897.

The professional side of the sport declined as the amateur side gained in popularity, though it has continued to this day. The most fascinating collision of the two worlds came after the famous 1908 Olympics. It was at this meeting that the distance of the marathon race became fixed at 26 miles 385 yards, or 42.195 km. Previous races had been about 25 or 26 miles. The 1908 Olympic race was started in Windsor Park, and the distance of the route taking them to the Olympic stadium (now the White City) was 26 miles. In view of the patronage of the event by Her Majesty Queen Alexandra, it was decided to take the runners round the track in front of the royal box, which brought it up to the distance mentioned.

The race itself was extremely dramatic. It was far more of a world-wide event than the meetings of 1896 and 1900. In the 1896 race, twelve of the sixteen starters were Greek, and in the Paris race there were several allegations that the winner, Michel Theato, only won because he knew short cuts through the streets of Paris. In 1908, however, there were fifty-six athletes, including men from South Africa, Canada and the leading European countries, as well as large teams from the host country and from the USA, which had naturally dominated the previous games in St Louis.

Everyone had his own favourite. The Italians were confident of the ability of Dorando Pietri, who had been unbeaten in several European races; the Canadians were quite sure that Tom Longboat, the Indian, would win, since he had broken the course record for the Boston Marathon by 5 minutes the previous year. The British press, with imperial confidence, predicted that their twelve entries (the maximum permitted number) would fill the first twelve places. The day was one of intense heat and humidity. Since the roads were mostly unmetalled and not closed to traffic, clouds of dust made breathing difficult. In spite of this, the leading British runners set off at a tremendous pace, cheered on by huge crowds. Tom Jack led through the first mile in 5 minutes 1 second, and at 5 miles he was still running fast (27.21) followed by two other British runners, Price and Lord, the South African Hefferon and the Italian Pietri. After that the pace started to slow. Jack stopped for refreshment and just before halfway, Price put in a burst and Lord dropped back. At 15 miles Hefferon broke away and Price gave up. The South African moved away to a 2-minute lead, then Tom Longboat made his effort, moving into second place and closing the gap slightly. However, the heat started to affect him, too; after stopping to walk and then getting going again, he collapsed totally at the 20 mile mark. The Englishman Appleby held second place briefly, then he too dropped out. Next it was Hefferon's turn to suffer. After the 20-mile mark he slowed to 8-minute miles, and his lead, at one time half a mile, dwindled rapidly. The little Italian, running slowly as he was, took the lead with a mile to go, but the effort completed his exhaustion. Queen Alexandra and the huge crowd in the stadium, estimated at 100,000, were aghast to see the leader turn the wrong way as he came on to the track. He was turned in the right direction, but collapsed. He got up unaided, and staggered another 50 yards before collapsing again. He continued to struggle towards the finish, only 200 yards away, then collapsed totally. At this moment another runner entered the stadium, the American John Hayes. Officials picked up Pietri and helped him across the line, with Hayes finishing 30 seconds later and Hefferon a close third. Pietri was at first declared the winner, then disqualified after a protest, on the grounds that he had received assistance, but he was given a gold cup by the Queen, for his courage. Hefferon protested, unsuccessfully, that Hayes, too, had been given unfair assistance, some of the Canadians said that Longboat had been drugged, and the British were forced to swallow their pride.

The effect of the public interest aroused by all this drama was soon seen on both sides of the Atlantic. In England the Polytechnic Harriers instituted an annual marathon, starting from Windsor Castle, which has been held ever since, and New York promoters staged the first 'World Professional' marathon championship, with a first prize of $3000 – worth at least ten times that amount today. It took the form of a series of two-man indoor marathons between Pietri, Hayes, Longboat and the English professional Alfred Shrubb, and the eventual winner was Tom Longboat.

In Europe, running became more and more the business of amateur clubs, and in spite of the great social divisions that existed between the wars, it has always been a classless sport. You cannot buy success in running, because the equipment is so basic. Certainly the university runners of the 1920s and 1930s had more chance of getting noticed, but the ordinary man had rather more chance of getting to the top in those days, because the standards were lower and the gulf between a fit young man and an international was not nearly as wide.

The next great impetus in the sport was the effect of the Finns – first Hannes Kohlemainen, then Paavo Nurmi, and then a dozen others, who between them dominated world distance running until just before the Second World War. It was Nurmi more than any other man who created the image of the lonely, dedicated distance runner. He was indeed a dedicated man who set himself standards far higher than anyone else. He trained all year round, and often ran to a time schedule because there was no one in the world to give him a race. He set world records at every official distancc from 1500m to 20km and won six individual gold medals in the Olympic Games, including winning the 1500m and the 5000m within 1½ hours in the Paris Olympics of 1924. Of many remarkable stories about him, the one which impresses me most concerns another aspect of those games. As Nurmi was already running four events, the selectors did not pick him for the 10,000m. To show what he could do, Nurmi ran a private time-trial at the same time as the race, and recorded 29 minutes 58 seconds, while in the stadium his fellow-countryman Ritola was winning the event in 30 minutes 23 seconds.

Nurmi exemplifies one kind of runner, the man who does it for the thing itself, regardless of what other people are doing. Although there is no room here to go into the histories of all the great figures in the world of running, I would like to tell you something of Emil Zátopek, because he is another kind of runner, a man who ran through sheer love of life, rather than for pride. He came from a small town in Czechoslovakia, which had no opportunities for sport, and he did not discover his talent for running until the age of eighteen, but by the age of twenty-four he was in the international class, and in the next two Olympics he won four gold and one silver medal, including the unequalled feat of winning the 5000m, the 10,000m and the marathon in the Helsinki Olympics. What was special about him? Simply that he believed that anything was possible. He did not accept the conventional bounds of training. He kept on trying new things, and if they worked he did more. In fact, he revolutionized training methods. He was competitive, obviously, but he was also friendly. He had and, as far as I know, still retains a curiosity about life. He would always talk to unknown runners and encourage them – which could be very off-putting in the middle of a race!

In the 1952 Olympic marathon, the English runner Jim Peters, the world record holder, set off at a tremendous pace. Zátopek, who was running his first ever marathon, started a little more slowly, but being a superb track runner he caught up with Peters when the latter slowed. As he caught up, Zátopek gave his cheerful smile and asked innocently, in English: 'Are we going fast enough?'

Zátopek's personality, the fame of his triple achievement and the spread of television gave running a post-war boost. His achievements also symbolize the world-wide nature of running, because the involvement of eastern Europe has become one of the most significant, though not the most beneficial, aspects of the sport in recent years. For all this, the runner remained a man apart from the rest of the population and the running woman was definitely a freak. Runners were heroes, certainly – no British runner has received as much admiration as did Roger Bannister in becoming the first man to break the 4-minute mile barrier, in 1954, but his success was mirrored in the number of spectators turning up at the White City rather than in the numbers joining athletic clubs. Bannister retired at the end of the 1954 season, after winning the European 1500m and defeating John Landy in the Vancouver Commonwealth Games, but he gave his name to an era. Britain was, for a few years, the dominant nation in distance running. Apart from Bannister, Gordon Pirie, Derek Ibbotson and Chris Chataway broke world records, Brian Hewson and Mike Rawson won the European 1500m and 800m, and Chris Brasher won the gold medal in the 1956 Olympic steeplechase. In the marathon Jim Peters brought the event into the modern era, reducing the world record from 2 hours 25 minutes to 2 hours 17 minutes. Peters's last race, however, though it has given him immortality in athletic history, was not the sort of race to inspire mass participation.

After his defeat by Zátopek, Peters was determined to win a major international title and his best chance was in the Commonwealth Games in Vancouver. Although he was clear favourite, he was always worried about his English team-mate, Stan Cox, who had given him several close races. He thus set off at a fast pace, not as fast as in Helsinki, but fast enough in view of the midday starting time and the hot weather. Although Cox tried to hang on, Peters went further and further in front, and when Cox dropped out with heat exhaustion at 24 miles, Peters had a lead of over a mile. This is the point where one does not know whether to admire his bravery or condemn his stupidity. He had no one out on the course, official or unofficial, to tell him how big his lead was. He could have walked most of the way back to the stadium and still won, but he kept ploughing on and his body temperature went on climbing. He came down the steep ramp into the stadium and as he turned on to the track his legs seemed to go from under him. When he picked himself up he was weaving from side to side, using the last vestiges of consciousness to keep his balance. After several falls he collapsed across what he thought was the finish line, unaware that the correct marathon finish was another 200m ahead, on the other side of the track. Luckily he was saved from death through heat exhaustion, but his story remains a permanent warning to officials and to runners about the dangers of running a marathon in the midday sun.

As the 1950s became the '60s, the expected things happened to the sport. More nations took part, world records were broken, new and exciting figures appeared on our television screens. The Australians Herb Elliott and Ron Clark, the New Zealanders Peter Snell and Murray Halberg broke their records and won their titles, only to be superseded by the new wave of runners from Africa. The Kenyans, Keino, Temu, Jipcho and Biwott, and the Ethiopians, Abebe Bikila and Mamo Wolde, seemed to be taking over from the effete and over-civilized nations of the western world. Only the Finns, who won the 1500m, 5000m and 10,000m in the 1972 Olympics, seemed to have innate ability to withstand the challenge.

Underneath all this, something totally unexpected was happening, the spread of a mass movement towards fitness. It had several preachers, but no leaders and no organization. It was a reversal of the trend towards more spectating, more television watching, more obesity and more heart disease, which had followed an unwavering upward curve for two decades, since the end of the Second World War.

Some point to President Kennedy's Fitness Award and some to Frank Shorter's marathon victory in the Munich Olympics as the starting points of the 'running boom', but I disagree.

If one has to fix a point when the movement began, it must be 1967, when Bill Bowerman, the Oregon University track coach, published, with two co-authors, a small book simply entitled *jogging*. It didn't even have a capital letter. Bowerman had been for many years a big figure in college running, in a country where the coach has a more lasting prestige than the athlete. His advocacy of jogging was noticed by the media and found eager acceptance amongst the general public. Bowerman himself acknowledges that he got the idea from the jogging club started in Auckland, New Zealand, by Arthur Lydiard. Where did Lydiard get the idea from? For him, it was a logical extension of his activities first as a competitive marathon runner and then as a highly successful coach. What was new was Lydiard's and Bowerman's enthusiasm for carrying the principles of serious athletics into the preaching of fitness for the ordinary non-competitive man and woman. The ideas had been around for a century, but runners had kept them to themselves, perhaps not thinking that anyone else would be interested.

The coincidence of two other factors prepared the ground for the seeds of the idea. The first was the increasing amount of leisure, and the second derived from the hippy movements of the 1960s. The personal goals of the western world, in the years after the Depression, lay in work and duty. The steady job, financial security, loyalty to the firm and to the country, were ideals which the hippy generation rejected. Very few people actually became hippies, but the youth of the 1960s grew up with different ideals, in which the needs of the individual took first place. In the 1970s we saw the development of what has been dubbed the 'me' generation. Self-realization is the goal and this is where running meets a need. Running is controlled by the individual, not by a set of regulations. You don't need a licence, a pitch, a referee or police permission. It's not taxable, but neither is it illegal, immoral or fattening. In a society where mere survival is no longer a purpose, running provides a purpose. Humans have something which no other animal has – a desire to achieve. We have been given this desire to do better, to achieve something more than just staying alive and in an age dominated by organizations, running is literally a life-line to the individual.

We can claim many other benefits for our sport – it is cheap, it is the best form of preventive medicine and it is accessible to all, but these things have always been true. Only when the ground is ready will the seeds germinate. I like to think that my own run across the USA in 1969 sowed a few seeds. When we crossed the state of Oklahoma we met the only registered athlete in the entire state – how many are there fifteen years later?

The jogging movement, like a healthy young shoot, grew in size without arousing any attention at all until the publication of Jim Fixx's *The Complete Book of Running* in 1977. Interestingly, Fixx's own interest in running started in 1968, following an injury which stopped him playing tennis. Eight years later he decided to write a book on running, because there was no comprehensive book available for the general reader and he needed the money. In his recent book, *Jackpot*, he quotes a woman he met at a party in Manhattan. When he told her what he was writing, she said, 'Who in the world will want to read a book about running?'

The Complete Book of Running came out in October 1977. It went straight into the *New York Times* bestseller list and stayed there for nearly two years. It earned the author $1.5 million in that time. Nothing arouses so much interest as a new way of making money. From the date that Fixx's book made the headlines, everyone became aware that running was a major American interest and, more than that, an interest which had rich commercial trimmings. A group of running enthusiasts in Oregon, including, I am glad to say, the pioneer Bill Bowerman, founded a running shoe company called Nike, which is now one of America's most successful companies and has made its founders into multi-millionaires.

Jim Fixx didn't invent the running boom, but he recognized it, and as a result he has become its patron saint. The public recognition, by making the sport fashionable, accelerated its growth. The numbers of runners entering in marathons, and the numbers of marathon races put on, showed a steady climb from the late 1960s to 1975. In October 1976 there was a massive turn-out – over 2000 runners – for the New York Marathon, and Jim Fixx's publisher wondered whether the book was going to come out too late – he thought that the running boom must have reached its peak! In the following three years the entries doubled each year, and were it not for the limitation of the field to 15,000 for safety reasons, applications would by now have topped the 100,000 mark.

What the Americans do today, the rest of the world does tomorrow. The year after Jim Fixx's book came out, I took some of my students to run in the Masters and Maidens Marathon, near Guildford. There were no prizes, and the course was tough, but I was amazed to find over 400 starters. I felt at the time that interest was undoubtedly growing. I had seen orienteering grow from nothing to a national sport in the previous decade, and I had seen the numbers in the English cross-country championships rise from 1000 to 2000 competitors, but I saw no reason to think that Britain would follow in America's footsteps in the road running boom. After all, we had been the world leader in running for a century, with the best organized network of athletic clubs and a busy year-round calendar of events. Was there room for more? The answer has been a resounding 'yes'. The *Sunday Times* Fun Run started in 1978 with 8000 runners and reached the 30,000 mark in 1983, but the distance was only 4km. Would the marathon fever prove as infectious as in America?

The man who gave us the answer was Chris Brasher, who bridged the gap between Olympic competition and mass participation by master-minding the first London Marathon in 1981. Over 7000 of us started from Greenwich on a wet spring morning. It was everything it promised to be – a festival of sport for its own sake, a celebration of human endeavour, enjoyed equally by those running, by the million Londoners out on the streets watching and the millions more watching on television. For many years I have run with serious runners, men and women with special talent for the sport, who have trained hard and achieved success. In that first London Marathon, and in the subsequent mass events, I have seen something quite different, the struggles of ordinary people, with no special talent, trying to win a battle with themselves. In many ways this is more inspiring, because none of them will ever achieve fame, or any sort of personal gain; they do it for its own sake, for their own satisfaction and self-respect.

The men and woman who have taken part in these races carry their achievements like a badge of courage. It is this status which more and more people all over the world are trying to achieve. It is for this reason that in the last year the number of marathon races in Britain has grown to 130, with over 100,000 people taking part. It is for this reason that the numbers of runners in the world's famous races have grown beyond belief.

The Boston Marathon, oldest and most famous of all, has imposed entry standards, but still has 10,000 runners, not to mention 2 million spectators. The Great North Run in Newcastle-on-Tyne now has 25,000 runners, the San Francisco Bay to Breakers 35,000, and the Stramilano in Milan over 50,000. Now that they have grown beyond counting, it is hard to say which is the biggest of all, but it was estimated that the Round the Bays race in Auckland, the cradle of jogging, had 78,000 runners, nearly half of them unofficial entries. This is three per cent of the population of New Zealand! The record for a 'women only' race is at present held by Dublin, where 8000 took part in a 10km race in 1983.

At the time of writing, there is no evidence that the boom has yet reached its highest level. The number of races being staged in 1984 exceeds that of 1983. The 'Corporate Cup' idea, borrowed from America, is bringing in more runners by staging events between businesses. The proportion of women running continues to rise. The last survey of leisure activities published in the Trade and General Index gave a figure of 2.8 million people in the United Kingdom who regularly run or take part in training. The equivalent figure in the USA is around 20 million – ten per cent of the population.

Can we predict what will happen next? The boom is bound to level out, and the numbers of runners will probably drop when more people diversify into other fitness activities such as cycling, hill walking and swimming. However, there is no doubt that we are witnessing a major shift in the pattern of society, which has already been reflected by a drop in heart-related diseases in the USA. The Americans used to be less fit and more obese than the British, and they had more heart attacks per 100,000 people. They have changed their life-styles, and they are reaping the benefits. This alone is bound to maintain the momentum of the movement.

If a pyramid has a broad base it is bound to have a high summit. There is, in fact, no break in continuity between the fully professional top-line performer and the twice-a-week jogger. The professional who runs 2 hours 10 minutes for the marathon is being chased home by some very serious amateurs running 2 hours 20 minutes. A few miles behind them is an army of men and women who have done enough training to run it in under 3 hours. They all share the same kind of problems, even though the motives of the top-liners may no longer be as noble as those of the also-rans.

Most of our motives are mixed. It is by no means impossible to run for fun and for profit and for glory and for patriotism at the same time. We start by running for fun and self-respect, and then the prestige gives an added incentive. The chance of representing one's country in an international event, and, above all, in the Olympic Games, is another spur. By the time the runner reaches the top national level he or she is already adopting a semi-professional attitude, in that life is organized around running. In that situation it is natural to accept offers of free equipment, travelling expenses to meetings, free accommodation and training camps. This has been the pattern of amateur sport for years.

After years of 'shamateurism', when athletes were paid money unofficially but declared themselves to be amateurs, we have moved very close to true professionalism. The establishment in 1981 of a separate road racing organization in America, offering cash prizes for races, caused the amateur authorities to move rapidly. In 1982 the International Amateur Athletic Federation, which governs the world's amateur authorities, sanctioned both the payment of money for advertising or endorsement of products, and the payment of cash for taking part in races. 1983 saw the first 'permit' meetings in track athletics. The money has to be paid into a 'trust fund', which can be used for training expenses, but the athlete remains eligible to run in the Olympic Games.

It cannot be long before the word 'amateur' disappears from the rule books. The logical situation in running, as in other sports, is that ninety-nine per cent of the sporting population will run for fun and prestige, and the handful of elite runners, who are so good that people will pay to watch them, will be paid whatever the market can stand. Where athletes are a big draw to television companies, they should be entitled to a share of the fee.

In the next few years, the country's best runners are going to be able to make the kind of money that is being enjoyed by the tennis players and the golfers. As in these sports, the money coming in from sales of equipment and clothing is sufficient to offer sponsorship and employment for those trying to reach the top, and continued commercial opportunities for those whose career has passed its peak.

Running is a life-long sport. At school level we offer competition and coaching, but perhaps just because it *is* so competitive, a lot of children turn away from it. In childhood we are less prepared to be second-best. In later life we realize that success and failure are relative, not absolute terms. We realize that success does not depend on being first across the finish line. In middle and old age, running has deeper satisfactions to offer. When you are young, you are only as good as your last race. One defeat brings gloom and depression. When you are older, every day's training is another brick in the fortress that we are building around ourselves, a protection against the forces of depredation and decay. Whether young or old, a champion or a back-of-the-bunch plodder, being a runner makes you a stronger person. Although the chapters on training, competition and tactics are written for the twenty-to-forty age group, the principles apply equally to older men and women. It is not your age or sex that dictates what you can do, but your fitness. The training put in by Joyce Smith at the age of forty-five would destroy the average young man!

The history of running is one of almost continual improvement. The only nineteenth-century record which still stands is that for the six-day race. The story is one of rising standards and harder training. The paths carved out by solitary pioneers are now followed by hundreds of others. It may be some comfort to realize that if you can break 15 minutes for 5000m or 2 hours 30 minutes for the marathon, you would, in 1906, have been a world record holder. It still requires just as much effort to run those times today.

3
Getting Going

'Afoot and light-hearted, I take to the open road', were Walt Whitman's words – well, now it is your turn.

You probably don't see yourself as one of those legendary figures of the last chapter, but the fact that you are reading this book shows that you are prepared to have a go at becoming a better runner. You are going on a journey of self-discovery. The person who says 'I go for a run twice a week and go to keep-fit on Tuesdays' is performing a holding operation, but not developing. He is on a par with the person who reads the Sunday papers but never goes to see a play or reads a new novel. Your body and your mind deserve more than this. As the Americans say: 'If you don't want to lose it, use it!'

If you want to get somewhere, you must have a goal. If it is running a marathon in a year's time, that's fine, but you will need something in the near future to motivate you. Find out from your local athletic club or jogging club what races there are in the next few months, and work towards those. Start with a distance you can be sure of completing, and try to improve the quality of your running. The schedules to follow are given in Chapter 4, but there are certain preliminary steps to be taken.

Self-criticism

Before your dreams carry you away, make an inventory of your physical attributes. Height does not matter – there are world class runners of 5 feet and 6 feet 4 inches. Long legs are a help in the shorter track distances – half mile and 1500m/mile, but a lot of long distance runners, particularly marathon runners, are short in the leg. A large upper body, unless it is on a correspondingly large frame, is a disadvantage, because you are carrying weight that is not going to help you run faster – maybe you should try the triathlon!

The two most important parameters are your height/weight ratio and your body-fat percentage. Within the normal height range of 5 feet 5 inches to 6 feet 1 inch, very few good distance runners weigh more than two pounds per inch of height. If you are 5 feet 10 inches (70 inches) high, you should weigh no more than 140 pounds (10 stones) to have a good chance. If you are a stone heavier than this, there is still hope, because you will lose weight as you get fitter, and this dictum only applies to runners of top national class anyway.

The body-fat thing is obvious. Not only are you carrying useless weight around, but the extra thickness of fat acts like thermal underwear: it insulates you, and the heat which you generate when running cannot escape. As your internal or 'core' temperature builds up, you will be forced to slow down. Pinching a fold of skin just above your navel gives you the answer. For a good runner the fold will be only a centimetre – well under half an inch – thick. If it is more than this, you have some to lose, but this loss is one of the benefits of serious training. If you are grossly overweight, with too much fat, maybe you should adjust your diet, and just stick to gentle jogging or cycling until your weight comes down. A lot of running when you are overweight places too much strain on your joints, so you are more likely to get injured than to get fit.

Whatever your ambitions, you can't change your genes, so you are confined within certain physical limits. That doesn't stop you improving, and it is the search for improvement that is important. A friend of mine, who seldom finishes more than halfway up the field in road races, says: 'I never let it worry me, because I reckon I always win the class for over-200-pound forty-two-year-olds.' The only person you are really competing against is yourself.

Pulse rate measurements. Count your pulse rate when you wake up in the morning, and count it again when at rest during the day. These two will give you some idea to your basic fitness. There is a very wide natural range of pulse rates, roughly 60 to 80 for adult men, 65 to 85 for women. This represents how hard your heart has to beat to keep your body supplied with oxygen at rest. As you become fitter, your heart becomes stronger and your muscles become more efficient in extracting oxygen from the blood, so your resting pulse will decrease. If your resting pulse is much higher than usual, and if there is no emotional reason for this, you are either getting unfit or you have something wrong with you. If your resting pulse is considerably higher than usual, do not go out training until it returns to its usual range.

When racing, it is an advantage if you can push yourself to a *high* pulse rate, because it means you can reach a very high effort level. However, for any single level of effort, say running a mile in 6 minutes, the *lower* your pulse, the better it is. One of the best ways of measuring your increase in fitness is to run a mile once a month. The speed should be easily within your compass, and the last lap should be run as levelly as possible. You should then measure your pulse rate for 30 seconds, one minute after stopping, 2 minutes after stopping and 3 minutes after stopping. As you get fitter, your pulse will drop more quickly after a hard run. You can use this as a guide when doing interval training (see Chapter 4), because you should always wait until your pulse has dropped to a plateau level of about 110 beats per minute before starting the next run. If you record 20 beats or more in a 10-second period, your pulse is still too high, and you should rest a little longer.

As you get older, your maximum pulse rate drops. Some

of the fitness assessment methods which rely on pulse rate may give a flattering result for the older person, because it is assumed that he has a maximum rate of 180 to 200 beats per minute, which is no longer the case.

Clothing

This depends on your temperament. If you believe that looking the part is the main thing, you should go out and buy a pair of training shoes, a pair of road racing shoes, a good track suit and a Gore-Tex rain suit. That will set you back about £250. If you have the legs for them, you can then buy a few pairs of fashion-designer shorts. To get the right T-shirts you will have to enter some exotic races such as the Bermuda or the Sea of Galilee Marathon. This will confirm your image, among your non-running friends at least, and you can be modest about your achievements without actually telling anyone how slow you are – 'Well, I was along way behind Grete Waitz!'

If you just want to get started in a modest way, I suggest that the only thing you need to buy is a pair of training shoes. It is worth going to a proper running store and trying on several of the well-known brands. The competition among shoe manufacturers is now so fierce that there are very few bad shoes on the market. Most of the shoes now sold are better than the best we could get twenty years ago. Even if your enthusiasm for the sport runs out after the first 100 miles you will still have a comfortable well-supported pair of casual outdoor shoes, so nothing is lost. Each firm has its own characteristics, and the sizes can be misleading, since there are European, Japanese, Korean and American shoes on the market. Try them with a thin sock. After a few weeks they will probably stretch slightly and you can then wear a thicker sock. You are looking for comfort, not fashion, so be sure that your feet can spread right out inside the shoe. Your big toe should just reach to the front of the shoe, but should be not pressing against it, otherwise you risk losing a toenail in a long race.

For the runner in a British climate, my advice is to have several layers of clothing – a singlet, a T-shirt, a fleecy long-sleeved top or track suit top, and a thin wind- and waterproof anorak. If you buy a track suit, avoid the very thin all-nylon ones, because they won't keep the wind out when you really need them to.

Apart from the training shoes, you don't have to have anything; when I won my first Amateur Athletics Association (AAA) championship at the White City, I was a hard-up student, and I wore a pair of jeans and a polo-necked sweater. When I was invited to join the British team to tour Russia I thought I had better buy myself a track suit. In the same way, if you start off with the minimum amount of clothing, you can treat yourself to a new top or a pair of shorts as you get more involved, or if you go to a special event. When I go out running now, I can select my Boston Marathon shorts, the singlet I swapped with a Frenchman and a track suit I won as a prize in a road race. When I want to do well, I have a special race kit, light in weight, fitting well but not too tightly, and I make sure that I have clean socks of the right thickness for my racing shoes.

If you are going to take racing seriously, you need the lightest pair of racing shoes compatible with comfort and support. The heavier person will need considerably more support, and there are shoes made for this purpose. It is not simply a matter of buying larger shoes, because your body weight goes up according to the *cube* of your height but shoe size only increases according to the *square* of your height. If you are racing over the country, you will need spikes, and you should have at least two lengths, 15mm and 9mm, so that you can cope with muddy or with frozen ground. If you are only competing occasionally at club level, and you don't need spikes for the track season, you would be better off with a lightweight pair of studs. The type of shoe with a lot of very short rubber studs is not a great deal of use in wet weather, because the spaces between the studs soon fill up with mud, and the same goes for the waffle sole, but they are fine in dry conditions.

Finding some company

With over 2 million joggers/trainers in the country, it is surprising how hard it can be to find a club to join. Going out by yourself or with a keep-fit enthusiast friend is all right to start with, but you will get a lot more fun, companionship and sense of purpose out of the sport if you are a member of a club. Start by going to a local road race or track meeting. If you don't know where to find these, ring up the sports desk of your local paper. They should be able to tell you where the races are. Other ways of finding out are through your local Area Sports Council, by buying *Running* magazine or *Athletics Weekly* from your local newsagent, or, if all else fails, by contacting the AAA offices in your part of the country (the addresses are given at the back of the book).

It is worth talking to runners from different clubs in your area to find out which is the most likely to give you what you need. Some athletic clubs concentrate more on road and cross-country races, others on track and field athletics. Some have jogging sections and some do not. Some clubs are mixed, others may be only for men or women. Some have a lot of strength in the veteran (over-forty) age group, while others ignore this category of competition. In my experience, what matters in a club is the enthusiasm and efficiency of the organizers, not the facilities. If you have a good bunch of people you will have a lot of fun, whatever the facilities. Having said that, the best club to join is probably the one closest to home, because you will use it more often.

The athletic club is, or should be, a voluntary association

of athletes dedicated to giving as much opportunity as possible to its members to take part in the sport. The club is the servant of its members, not their master. However, there are times when the club may make demands on you which do not always fit in with your needs as an individual. What do you do when you are building up for a race in three weeks' time and the club asks you to run for them in a road relay, which doesn't fit in with your plans? My advice is to be flexible about your plans. When you join a running club, you will find that the more you give it, the more it will give you. If you haven't experienced the feeling of being in a successful club team in a road or cross-country race, you have missed a great experience. By being a member of a good team, you can become greater than you are as an individual. Later in your career, when you are going for some important individual title, you will get support and understanding from your fellow members if they know that you have paid your dues in the past.

Time and place. Once you have got yourself tied up with a group of athletes, you will be able to get out with some training companions at least twice a week. I am against training in company all the time, because you tend to run always at the speed which suits other people, rather than the speed which is right for you. I have seen several promising athletes discouraged by getting burned off in club training runs for which they were not really ready.

You should decide what training *you* want to do and then see who else will do it with you. The long slow runs can obviously be done as a group – you can talk as you run, make your excuses for your last race and make plans for the next one. Hill training or interval training sessions go well with a group, too. In this case it doesn't matter if some run slower than others, as long as you have the same recovery time. For example, I can have a group of ten runners doing interval 600m runs, with a 3-minute interval between each. The best runners in the group will be running them in, say, 98 seconds each, the slower ones in just over 110 seconds, so the faster runners will have 10 seconds longer to recover, which makes very little difference. The better runners may do eight of these in a session, and the less fit runners may do the first four, then come in for the sixth and the eighth.

There are times when you will have to run on your own, and all runners have to get used to this. Fundamentally, you are always on your own, and unless you can learn to push yourself, using your own motivation, you are not going to get very far.

The best time to run is when you have the most time to spare. This may mean before breakfast, in the lunch-hour or after work. Personally, I don't function well first thing in the morning, and if I do go out at that time, it is just a loosening-up session, to work off the effects of the previous day. Unless you have a long lunch-hour, directly after work is the best time to train, and you should aim to go out straight away, without eating. One cannot train properly within an hour of eating, and two hours afterwards is a better time. If you are going to train hard at six o'clock, you must make sure you have had some lunch, otherwise your fuel reserves may be run down too much and your training will suffer – and so will you!

A lot of thought should be given about the place in which you do your training. The nicer the place, the more likely you are to keep going there. Variety is important. I like to have enough variety in my training so that I repeat each session only every two weeks. I suggest that to satisfy all the needs of the runner, you should have the following venues:

1 A short (1 to 2 miles) road circuit, preferably with street lights, for time trials and repetitions

2 Circular courses, road or cross-country, of roughly 3

miles, 5 miles and 8 to 10 miles. The exact distance need not be known

3 A flattish grass area, e.g., a park or cricket ground, preferably over half a mile round, for speed and interval work

4 A running track for timed interval work

5 At least one course on soft going, e.g., sand, forest path, for getting away from the road

6 A hill climb area, not too steep – about 1 in 10 (ten per cent) – but long enough to give you over 30 seconds of running. If you have no hills, use an overpass or a multi-storey car park

7 Some nice rugged countryside for long weekend runs

8 A gym or sports hall for indoor training when the weather is really bad

9 Some rough going, e.g., sand dunes, plough, for resistance training.

Even if you haven't got all of these, trying to find them will force you to look at your neighbourhood with new eyes.

Coping with the weather

Wet weather. Within any week of training, it is quite allowable to swap the days around; so you can just put on a waterproof suit and do a slow run, or you can take one of your rest days. If the schedule demands that you *have* to go out and do something useful, then put on a waterproof anorak, including hood, and keep as dry as possible during the warm-up (the same applies to racing in the wet). Synthetic materials, particularly polypropylene, absorb less moisture than cotton, so they do not get as heavy and clinging. If I have to train in wet weather, I stick to road running, put on a thin nylon anorak, and do either a fast continuous run or a fast Fartlek run (see Chapter 4). There is a significant point to remember when doing a long run in wet conditions, which is that hypothermia can result from the continued evaporation of water from wet clothing. Every time a molecule of water turns from liquid to vapour it draws a little bit of heat from the skin, and this can have a very nasty effect on a long run. If you *have* to go out, wear something that doesn't cling to the skin, and, if necessary, come home after the first 10 miles, dry off and go out again in dry kit. Skin, thank goodness, is waterproof, and you won't shrink.

Cold weather.

> If you must go and climb Himalayas
> Remember your grandmother's prayers:
> You must begin with wool next to the skin,
> And then layers and layers and layers.

This is still true, and the outer layer should be windproof yet 'breathable', of the Gore-Tex type. In less intense cold, concentrate on keeping your head and hands warm. There is nothing wrong with wearing a woolly hat in a race. A lot of energy is expended in keeping the body warm, and the head is a major source of heat loss, so you may well perform better with a hat – it has virtually no effect on weight or wind-resistance. In ice and show you will obviously have to take a great deal of care with your footwear. Soft snow is fine for resistance training (see Chapter 4), but for packed snow short spikes may be needed. If I have to run on snowy roads at night I usually wear boots with Commando soles.

An excuse for not running in the cold is, 'the cold air gets into your chest'. In fact, the air is warmed as it goes down the bronchial tubes, and a careful study carried out recently showed no evidence of any harm done to the lungs in this way. I have suffered mild discomfort from the inside of my nose freezing up, but that is all. In cold weather you can always put on more clothing, which may slow you down, but it need not stop you.

Hot weather. Overheating is a problem for distance runners, but don't confuse heat discomfort with fatigue. Most British runners get bothered when the temperature goes over 70 degrees Fahrenheit in low humidity. You can go through the rare British spell of heat by cutting down slightly on the very long runs and drinking plenty of fluid before and after running. In real heat, of the kind found in Arizona or in the tropics, you may have to train only in early morning and late evening, when it is below 80 degrees, and even then you have to take drinks every 3 or 4 miles to prevent dehydration and the ensuing heat exhaustion.

When first going to a hot country, you should take precautions against sunburn, and you should not try to carry on the same training programme as in a more temperate climate. In the first week, run half the daily training distance, and take as much liquid as you can comfortably hold in the hours after training. It will probably take you a week to acclimatize, and then you can start to move back to your normal training programme. White clothing is best in the heat and cotton is better than synthetic material.

A racing strategy

You probably have some idea about which running event you prefer, but even if you are convinced that you are a slow runner who can hope only to perform well in long races, there is still a lot of choice left open to you – 10-milers or marathons on the road, cross-country, orienteering or fell running. You must realize that until you are fit you cannot really tell where your talents lie. Even if you are a natural marathon runner, you cannot do well in the event unless you have a lot of training behind you. Another thing to bear in mind is the level of competition. If you are a girl who, after two months' running, can run a mile in 6 minutes, you might come in the first three in a local fun run, but if you went in for an inter-club track race you might be half a lap behind everybody else. With the same ability, if you did enough training you might place well up in the county cross-country championships and have a chance of winning a half-marathon race. In the last few years we have seen several runners, brought into the sport by the running boom, go rapidly to the top. A notable example is Sarah Rowell, who was a good class hockey player. She decided to take up marathon running and after six months' training she ran 2 hours 54 in the 1982 London Marathon. Encouraged by this, she got down to serious training, raced a handful of times over shorter distances, and then ran 2 hours 39, placing ninth woman in the 1983 London race. In one year, she moved from being a complete unknown to representing Britain, and in July 1983 she won an international title by winning the first ever women's marathon in the World Student Games in Edmonton.

My advice for the beginner is to start modestly with distances you know you can complete, at a local level. As you get fitter, enter for longer events and see how you get on. Give yourself a chance to recover from one race before entering the next – two or three weeks between each is advisable to start with. After six months, make an honest appraisal of your progress, decide which events your prefer, and then choose an event a month or so ahead and train specifically for that.

Keeping records

The most valuable thing you will gain from running is self-knowledge. Keeping a training diary is a tremendous aid in this process. You can go into as much detail as you like, but you will find it very helpful to record the following information in a way that will enable you to see the pattern by glancing through it: miles covered; type of training (e.g., steady run, intervals; details (times and distances); going (e.g., road, track); weather; how I felt.

This information should be kept in a concise form, and the total miles run per week and per month can be shown. By having it all close together, it will be obvious if you are doing too much, because the 'how I felt' column will have a row of 'tired', 'hard work', 'leg strain', 'exhausted at finish', and so on. One or two such comments a week may just be a sign that you are putting in some good work, but if they pile up it is likely that you will either get injured or pick up some minor infection.

More information can be got by keeping a race commentary book. This is only for the really introspective, because it will contain the kind of things that athlete and coach talk over after each race or each really searching training session. One analyses the performance, and how the runner felt. One considers the weak points and the strong points. For example, if you attack and pass several opponents up a hill, and they come past you again towards the finish, you can note your good performance on the hill as a strong point, but your lack of pace judgement or lack of finishing speed as a weak point. You then know what needs correcting in the next few weeks of training.

Training and racing records become more and more valuable to you as time goes on, but it is important to keep them right from the start, because then you can see how you have improved (or otherwise!) in the course of a season or two. As you get fitter you take your physical condition for granted, but by looking in the diary you can see what sort of a person you were at the beginning. The diary is, of course, particularly valuable in planning the year ahead, but I have left this until the last chapter when I hope you will know a lot more about running, and about yourself.

4
The Basics of Training

I am assuming that anyone reading this book has already gone through the basic stages of being 'just a jogger'. I would define a jogger as someone who is covering not more than 10 miles a week *and* whose speed is less than 8 miles per hour (7.5 minutes per mile). Thus, a fit games-player who goes out twice a week and runs 4 miles in 25 minutes is something more than a jogger, and so is somebody who is covering 5 or 6 miles at a stretch, even if the miles are slow ones.

The first stage is moving from jogger to runner. This implies, first of all, a commitment to running for its own sake. Whereas the jogger is only jogging for the sake of fitness, the runner is out to improve his running, in terms of being able to run further and faster than before. The sensible way to improve upwards is to improve the quantity first and then the quality of the running.

Assuming that our athlete is already running over 10 miles a week, and can run at least 3 miles non-stop, the next phase is to move up to a regular 30 miles a week. This, I would suggest, is the minimum basic mileage for any serious distance runner. There may be weeks, when, because of pressures of work or family, you simply cannot get out often enough, and the mileage may drop to 20, but if you can get up to 30 miles a week and maintain that, you will have the basis for successful performance at a wide variety of distances. If you are starting from a basis of 10 to 12 miles a week, done in three or four outings, you should progress along the following lines:

Schedule 1. The Build-up to 30 Miles per Week

Week 1	15 miles	(3 miles; 4 miles; 3 miles; 5 miles)
Week 2	15 miles	(3; 4; 3; 5)
Week 3	18 miles	(4; 5; 4; 5)
Week 4	18 miles	(4; 4; 4; 6)
Week 5	21 miles	(5; 5; 5; 6)
Week 6	21 miles	(5; 5; 4; 7)
Week 7	23 miles	(5; 3; 5; 3; 7)
Week 8	24 miles	(5; 4; 5; 3; 7)
Week 9	25 miles	(5; 5; 5; 3; 7)
Week 10	28 miles	(5; 3; 5; 3; 5; 7)
Week 11	30 miles	(5; 3; 6; 4; 5; 7)
Week 12	30 miles	(5; 3; 6; 4; 4; 7)

You can see that we are progressing in three ways – the number of runs per week, the total mileage and the distance of the longest run. For the latter you will need to put aside about an hour, so this will probably be at weekends, but most of the other sessions will be 40 minutes or less. This means that you will be able to fit the runs into your normal daily life without too much trouble, as discussed in Chapter 3. The exact distance of each run does not really matter – they can be estimated from milestones, from an Ordnance Survey map or from driving round in the car, or simply by how long it takes you, as long as you have a rough idea of your minutes per mile. It *is* important that you have different places to run, with different types of going.

What about pace? In the first few weeks I suggest that you do not worry at all about increasing your speed. You may well find, if you get into the habit of timing yourself round certain courses, that your times will improve without extra effort, just because you are getting fitter, but *don't* make every training session a personal record attempt – it only needs a few failures for you to get fed up with the whole business. I like to measure my progress, or decline nowadays, by timing myself over certain courses every three or four weeks, and I pick a day when I am feeling good and the weather conditions are not too unfavourable.

With the increase in number of days running per week, working up to six, you are steadily becoming more of a runner. The hardest part, initially, is going to be building up the distance of the long run. The important thing is to give yourself plenty of time, so that you can slow down, or walk if necessary, but you still have time to complete the course.

What about races? After six weeks on this plan, there is no reason why you should not try a race – any distance up to 10 miles. Don't expect too much, but have a go and see how your time comes out. If you *do* race, give yourself one or two days of rest or very light jogging (2 miles of shuffling) before returning to your regular programme. After following the twelve-week programme you could even tackle a half-marathon. Whether you do or not, you are now fully equipped to tackle the next upwards step.

Interval training

The 30 miles a week plateau is one that you should stay on for some time. Within this framework you can run up to 10 miles in a single day, and yet the over-all load on the body is unlikely to be great enough to cause injury or breakdown. It will give you enough of a background of stamina to take part in races up to the half-marathon distance, and, if you adjust the balance of the training in the right way, you can reach a very high standard in middle distance races, and, indeed, even at the 5000m and 10,000m distances. There is a time, as we shall see, when you may want to increase the distance you are running, but if, like most people, you can afford only a little time for training each day, you will do well to exploit the opportunities of 30 miles a week before going further. Of course, if your real reason for running is to work off tension or to get away from your job or your family, you will do better to skip this bit and to go on to the section on 'increasing mileage' on page 87.

Speeding up. Over the last couple of years I have received a good many letters from people who feel that they have stagnated, after making steady improvements in their first year of running. They have run in races and they have done time-trials, and they find that they are stuck in a groove, able to run only at a certain maximum speed – say 7 minutes per mile. They are basically fit, but they want to be faster, yet they have neither the time nor the inclination to increase the number of hours they spend on training. This is a familiar state of affairs. It is the situation which confronts every fit nineteen-year-old when he finds that he is not automatically getting stronger and faster every year. In the world of track running we have evolved a whole series of different schedules, finely tuned for athletes at different levels in different events, but they are all based on the same principle, now known as the 'interval training' system.

Interval training relies on the observed effect that our cardiovascular system gets the most benefit from training when our pulse rate is beating at between three-fifths and four-fifths of maximum. This has the great advantage of being true for all levels of fitness. An unfit man may need to run only at 8 minutes per mile to get his pulse up to this range, but a really fit person may be running at well under 5 minutes per mile without going out of the upper range. The principle does not state how long you should keep it up – that depends on how long it takes you to get tired. It isn't necessary to keep on taking your pulse or to buy an expensive pulse meter, because your inner feelings are a reliable guide, and can easily be checked. Run 200 yards at a comfortable speed, then stop and take your pulse for a short period of time – only 15 or 20 seconds, because it drops as soon as you stop running. Now do another 200 yards at a speed faster than comfortable, but which you would describe as 'not very hard', then stop and take your pulse again. Repeat the process for 200 yards at a 'hard pace' and then, having given yourself time to get your breath back and stop feeling tired, run 200 yards 'very hard' and take your pulse after each run.

Unless you are a trained athlete or a fanatic, it is unlikely that your last run will have got you up to your maximum heart rate.

For someone fit and under the age of 30, with a maximum heart rate of around 200 beats per minute, the results will appear something like this:

Table 1. Increase in Heart Rate

Perceived effort (over 200 yards)	*Heart rate* (beats per minute)
easy	110
comfortable	120
not very hard	130
fairly hard	140–150
hard	155–165
very hard	170–180
intolerably hard	190 plus

For this person, the best training effect will be obtained when running at a speed which is faster than 'comfortable' without being 'very hard'.

The reason behind this is that the heart gets the most benefit when its own blood supply is at a maximum, which is within this range, and it also seems likely that running in this range places the maximum demand on the muscle enzyme systems which are most in use in 'steady-state' running.

What we are trying to improve at this stage of training is not your flat-out sprinting speed, but your miling speed.

The drawback is that it is harder work than just running along easily, as you did in the early weeks of training. You have to start pushing yourself beyond the 'comfortable' stage, but I am assuming that you are prepared, even eager, to do this.

In the first instance you should introduce only one of these 'interval' or 'quality' sessions a week, and the distance of the fast runs should be pretty modest, say 120 yards or metres. Let's make the first session ten runs of this distance, written in the schedule as: 10 × 120m. After each fast run, which is run at a pace you feel is 'fairly hard', you should walk until your breathing returns to normal and your pulse rate returns to less than three-fifths of its maximum. (This means below 120 beats per minute for most people, or no more than 20 beats in 10 seconds.)

An increase in pace like this places considerably more strain on the muscles and joints than easy running, so you should precede the fast runs with at least a mile of easy jogging, plus stretching and loosening exercises.

Where should you do these sessions? Anywhere will do, but firm, level grass or hard sand is the ideal, because there is less jarring when running at speed.

How many should you do? There is no limit. Emil Zátopek, the great Czech runner, used this method, and at one time he was running as many as forty fast bursts of 400m each in a single training session. It is a good thing to increase the length of the burst as you get more used to the system – it gives better results, as long as you don't go too far.

That, then, is the key to how much you should do. The quantity and quality of the training that you undertake depends on what you *have* been doing, and in its turn it will determine what you *can* do in the future. By progressive training we go from the possible to the impossible. Let us assume that you are training five days a week, with steady unpressured running.

The first step will be to introduce quality training on one day a week. In the early stages you will need to walk or jog for about the same distance as you have run fast, to give yourself time to recover. A 5-mile session might therefore consist of one mile steady running to warm up, then twelve fast bursts of 200m, each followed by 200m of walking or slow jogging, amounting to a total of 3 miles, and then another mile of steady running to 'warm-down'. Out of a total of 5 miles, only 1½ miles were actually fast work. As you get fitter you might be able to cut down on your recovery jog and put in a bit more quality work, but even so the fast work is not likely to total more than half the entire distance run, and it will form less than ten per cent of the total week's mileage. Nevertheless, this small amount of work will be harder than anything you have done before, and will mark a real change in your state of fitness.

The beauty of interval training is that the principle applies no matter how long the bursts or where you do them. A pleasantly disguised form of interval training is the Swedish Fartlek system, where both the length of the bursts and the length of the recovery period are left to the individual. Fartlek is typically done on woodland paths or playing fields, but it can equally well be done on a stretch of road, a treadmill, a beach, inside a sports hall or in an airport building. Its advantage is variety, but its drawback is that it is difficult to measure progress. If you are running away from the track, the 'time interval' session is the next most disciplined form. A typical session would be: 2 × 2 minutes fast, 3 minutes slow; then 4 × 1 minute fast, 2 minutes slow; then 4 × 30 seconds fast, 1 minute slow.

Having introduced quality training at first on one day a week, and then on two days a week, the pattern of the training might appear as follows:

Schedule 2. Jogger-into-Runner: Two-Week Sample Schedule

WEEK 1

Sunday: Easy run, 5 to 8 miles

Monday: Rest or 2 to 3 miles jogging or other sport

Tuesday: 1 mile warm-up, then 6 × 300m at a brisk pace, with 300m walk/jog recovery; then 6 × 200m fast, with 200m walk/jog recovery; warm-down. Total 5 to 6 miles

Wednesday: Easy run, 3 miles

Thursday: Warm-up, then Fartlek or untimed interval training, including 8 × 200m fast and 6 × 150m fast, with equal distance walk/jog recovery. Total 5 miles

Friday: Rest

Saturday: Long warm-up, then 1 mile fast, timed. Ten minutes' rest or walking, then another timed mile. Warm-down

WEEK 2

Sunday: Easy run, 5 to 8 miles

Monday: Rest, jog or other sport

Tuesday: Warm-up, then 2 × 800m brisk speed, 3 minutes recovery; 4 × 400m fast, 2 minutes recovery; 4 × 200m fast, 1 minute recovery

Wednesday: Easy pace, 3 miles

Thursday: Fartlek or speed work on grass, as previous Thursday

Friday: Rest

Saturday: Race, fun run, time-trial, mountain climb or adventure.

Total mileage for two weeks: approx. 55.

You will notice that at the end of the first week there is a sneaky time-trial session. If you sincerely want to get better you have got to go out and measure yourself regularly, and this is a simple way of doing it. It doesn't even matter if your mile is not measured precisely, as long as you use the same course week after week, year after year. This way you can't fool yourself. I have a stretch in Devon, along the Barnstaple to Bideford road, which I have been using for time-trials for over twenty years. It has plotted my improvement and my decline and now it is doing the same for my children and my protégés. I still don't know exactly how far it is, and I hope I never shall because it might disillusion me, but it gives me that vital piece of information – am I getting any better?

Building strength. By strength I mean just that, in particular strength in the legs. You can build this up by weight training, if you have the equipment available, but for most of us it is cheaper and easier to use our own bodyweight as the resistance. It also has the advantage that, since you are running while doing your strength training, the blood supply to your leg muscles should develop along with the muscles.

The best way to strengthen leg muscles is to run up hills. I think that it is common sense to carry out the hill running at about the same speed as that at which you race, so this dictates that the hill should not be too long or too steep. A gradient of between 1 in 5 and 1 in 10 will do, with the running time somewhere between 45 seconds and 3 minutes so that you get a prolonged training effect. The total session should take as long as one of your normal runs, including the warm-up, but the total distance run will be slightly shorter.

The technique when running up hills in training should be to do it vigorously, with plenty of arm and leg drive, which means a good knee lift. This makes your muscles work really hard. By contrast, when you are running up hills in a race, you should try to shuffle up the hills, with short steps and little knee lift. In training you should be trying to work hard, to get the maximum response from your body, but in races the emphasis should always be on economy of effort.

If you want to get tougher still there are all sorts of interesting and masochistic variations in strength training. You can do your hill running up sand dunes or ploughed fields; you can wear army boots or a weighted jacket while doing so, or you could imitate the young Scottish 400m runner, Lindsay Macdonald, by dragging behind you a rope attached to a motor tyre. Indoors, you can get the same benefits by running on an inclined treadmill, or by pedalling against resistance on an exercise bicycle. All these forms of training are sometimes referred to as 'resistance training', for obvious reasons. They are particularly useful to the middle distance runner, who relies a great deal on leg power, but they are important to everyone, and should form a part of the training before the racing season begins. Because it is hard work, it may take a couple of days to recover, and so some athletes abandon this type of work in the racing season.

When you have become adjusted to including quality work in the form of interval training or Fartlek, you can introduce hill training instead of one of the interval sessions, once every two weeks. If your regular runs happen to include a lot of hilly courses, you will already be getting the leg strengthening benefit, but the more you tend to do your steady running on the flat, the more necessary it is to include hill work. Not only the legs benefit; it will make a lot of difference to the supporting muscles in the back and the abdomen, which become very important in the last stages of a distance race.

Putting on the pressure. Once you have got used to running 25 to 30 miles a week, you can start introducing first one and then two interval-type sessions a week, so that after about four weeks you are on to the type of schedule shown on page 63. Introducing hill running will make the schedule a little harder, though without taking up any more time. Where do you go from there? If you are going on to run half-marathons or full marathons seriously, you will need to graduate to the schedules in Chapter 6, but if you are intending to run cross-country or road races in the 5 to 7 miles (8 to 11km) range, then this schedule will suffice for your first season of competition. It will even fit you quite well for running track races in the 1500m to 5000m range to start with, since it contains both speed and stamina work; but if you want to get serious about track racing you should go on to the schedules in Chapters 9 and 10.

However, let me assume that you are an adult runner of moderate ability and some ambition, whose aim is 'to be a better runner'. Should you aim to improve your stamina, your speed, your flexibility or your leg strength? I suggest that you pick on one thing at a time, and the thing which you pick on will depend on your priorities and on your attitude to the sport. If you just like running, and can afford the time, then you can add a few miles per week of steady running to each session, until you move up to 40 or even 50 miles a week. On the other hand, if you are the busy, aggressive type-A achiever, who wants to extract the best out of every available moment, you can follow the High Pressure Plan which worked so well for me when I was an aggressive, busy, type-A achiever. This is the system which I worked out, with the help of friends at university, using the interval methods popularized by Franz Stampfl, the English cross-country tradition and the 'rugged' approach of the Australians and New Zealanders.

The basis of it is that once you have become accustomed to a certain weekly mileage, you gradually intensify each session, cutting down on the rest periods and increasing the proportion of fast work to slow work. As we approach closer to simulating racing conditions, it becomes tougher mentally, but in the physical sense it is very good training, because it is very specific to the event for which you are training. The great Sydney Wooderson achieved times of 4 minutes 6 seconds for the mile and 1 minute 49 seconds for the half-mile in the 1930s, on a training volume of about 20 miles a week. His coach was Albert Hill, an Olympic champion who had himself been coached by Sam Mussabini, and their methods were based on short high-pressure time-trial sessions over a variety of distances. The drawback was that he could only manage a few good races each season, but he was very successful. My view is that, for all serious distance runners except the marathon men, quality usually outweighs mere quantity of training.

The specific type of session which I would recommend for the ambitious runner is the 'repetition' session. This is really a variant of interval training, in which the bits of fast work are far longer and are followed by equally lengthy rest periods. The distance run depends on the event for which you are training, as does the number of repetitions. For a middle distance runner the session would be repetitions of 600m to 1200m, with three to four repetitions per session; for a 5000m runner the distance would be 4 × 1200m to 1600m; and for the man aiming for distances around 10,000m the 'reps' would be a mile to 1½ miles in length (1600m to 2400m), done four to six times.

The other ways in which you can put pressure on yourself are by speeding up your steady running and adding just one more fast burst to your Fartlek sessions, or just one hill run in that workout. This will result in a modified version of the schedule on page 63, which will now look like this:

Schedule 3. High-Pressure Plan: Two-Week Sample Schedule

WEEK 1

Sunday: Jog 2 miles, then 5 to 6 miles at brisk pace

Monday: Warm-up, then 3 miles fast, then 1 mile warm-down
Tuesday: 1 mile steady, 8 × 1 minute fast, 1 minute slow; then 8 × 30 seconds fast, 30 seconds slow. Total: 5 miles approx.
Wednesday: 3 to 5 miles easy or brisk, as you feel
Thursday: Hill training, 12 to 20 × 120m up a 1 in 10 slope, 1 mile jog
Friday: Rest
Saturday: Race or warm-up plus 2 × 2 miles time trial (6 to 8 minutes rest)

WEEK 2
Sunday: As previous Sunday, but different course
Monday: 5 miles brisk Fartlek
Tuesday: Warm-up, then 4 × 1500m road circuit (5 minutes rest)
Wednesday: 4 to 6 miles, steady at first, then with fast strides, 50 to 100m
Thursday: Warm-up, then 10 × 200m (45 seconds recovery), then 10 × 150m
Friday: Rest
Saturday: Race

Total mileage for two weeks: approx. 65

Progressive training

The kind of training outlined above is going to require quite a lot of will-power, particularly if you are doing it on your own. Over a period of three months maximum this can be kept up, gradually putting in a little bit more fast work every two weeks, or else trying to improve on the timed bits every time a suitable session comes up in the two-week cycle. Ideally, this programme should be aimed at a particular race; and the races which precede the big day should be regarded as part of the training. When you come down to it, the best preparation for racing is racing, because it is a matter of concentrating one's efforts into a fairly short space of time. Your body has to learn to function at maximum efficiency for the 20 or 30 or 40 minutes of a race – not for the hour or more of a training session.

There is a saying, 'training builds you up, racing breaks you down'. It is only a partial truth. All training, at least all training worthy of the name, puts some strain on the system, and really hard training or racing *will* break you down, in terms of exhausting the body's fuel reserves, causing dehydration, higher temperatures and, possibly, swollen joints. However, unless you expose the body to stress, it will not adjust to it. The art of progressive training lies in exposing the body to not too much stress, so that it can recover in time for the next hard session. In the first schedules the stress of coping with regular daily running is quite enough, and the total amount is increased gradually. Then we move on to the schedule on page 63, where there is good quality training every other day, and a day of light training allows for recuperation. In the schedule on page 68, there are still hard sessions only on Tuesday, Thursday and Saturday (or whichever is the race day), but the assumption is made that the athlete is recovering more quickly, so the Monday and Wednesday sessions, and every part of the Sunday run, are done at such a speed that they are giving a real training benefit.

When you come to races, you will benefit from them as long as you give yourself enough rest afterwards for the body to make the necessary adjustments. I have known athletes go into a routine of racing two or three times a week for four or five weeks, and getting better and better because they are giving themselves the necessary rest after each race, and rising up to a higher and higher level. You have to learn by experience how to do this as your training becomes progressively harder. I find that it is mentally possible to keep the pressure on oneself for three months, but after that it is advisable to have a week or ten days of easy unpressurized running and plan a fresh campaign with different targets. To retain the enjoyment of the challenge, one needs to switch the emphasis at different times of the year. For the average runner, there are some ideas about this on page 93 and for the more purposeful distance man it will be a matter of what some people call 'periodization', with probably a competitive peak in both summer and winter, in cross-country, road or track, and a pre-season build-up phase before each period of competition. These are dealt with in the appropriate chapters.

5

What Goes on Inside

Imagine a man walking along a road at a comfortable pace, say three miles per hour. As he walks, his leg and buttock muscles contract and relax, moving his legs. The muscles of his back and the abdomen are being used to keep his trunk upright, the muscles of his chest are being used in breathing and the muscles of his arms and shoulders are being used to maintain his balance. Even his neck muscles are being used a little, to keep his head balanced. If he breaks into a trot, all these muscles will have to work a little harder, but particularly the leg muscles. To keep the leg muscles supplied with oxygen he will have to breathe more rapidly and his heart will have to beat faster, so that the blood can carry the oxygen at a faster rate. The heart, of course, is made of muscle, so it too will have to work harder and will use up more energy.

Where does the energy come from? It comes originally from food, but we all carry energy stores about with us. There are minute amounts of chemical energy, in the form of high energy phosphates, in the muscle fibres. As soon as these are used up, which is in a matter of seconds, they must be regenerated by burning up glucose. There is glucose in our blood, and as this is used up it is replaced from the glycogen stores. Every muscle has its own reserve of muscle glycogen and in addition there is a sort of 'general reserve fund' of glycogen in the liver.

For some evolutionary reason there is about enough glycogen in the liver to enable the average athlete to run for 18 miles flat out. If he is running at a pace slower than flat out, more and more of his energy will come from the breakdown of fat. The energy stored in our fat reserves is enough to keep us going for weeks – it was what primitive man relied on to keep him alive through hard times. We also get a certain amount of energy from protein breakdown, but this is still a matter of controversy. The supply of energy from the fat and protein source is pretty slow. If you are walking, then you can be supplied with calories from fat breakdown at a rate fast enough to maintain a constant level of blood glucose, but the faster you run the faster you will eat into your glycogen stores.

What determines how fast you run? It depends largely on how much oxygen you can get to your muscles. If you have an efficient and well-developed heart and blood system you may be able to absorb, via your lungs, over 5 litres of oxygen per minute. In order to absorb this much oxygen, the amount of actual air passing in and out of your lungs may be as much as 150 l per minute. Taking in this much oxygen allows you to burn up a lot of glucose and produce a lot of energy, which enables your leg muscles to drive you along. How efficiently you use this energy depends on your build, your style and your weight. If two people have an equal oxygen intake, the lighter man will be able to go faster. For this reason, oxygen intake is always expressed relative to body weight, in millilitres of oxygen per kilogram of body weight per minute. If two men have heart and lung systems of the same size and efficiency, with equally powerful chest muscles for moving air in and out, they will be able to take in the same amount of oxygen per minute – let us say 5 l. If one man is small, weighing 50kg (110 pounds) his oxygen intake will be $\frac{5 \times 1000}{50}$ millilitres per kilogram per minute (because there are 1000ml in a litre). This oxygen intake of 100ml/kg/min. would be phenomenally high, and anyone possessing it would probably be a world record holder. A 75kg (165 pounds) man with a 5 l/min. oxygen intake would have a figure of 66.7ml/kg/min., which would make him a good but not exceptional athlete. World-class distance runners usually have the ability to take in between 70 and 80ml/kg/min.

Can you improve your oxygen intake? The size of your chest and lungs cannot vary, but, provided your chest muscles are strong enough, getting the air in and out is no problem. The pumping capacity of the heart is much more important. Over years of training the runner's heart, like any other muscle, becomes larger and stronger. It is capable of pumping more blood at each stroke. For this reason the pulse rate, measured at rest, will get lower as you get fitter (see also Chapter 3).

Other changes take place in your leg muscles as you continue to train. The capillaries, minute blood vessels which connect arteries to veins, supply your muscle fibres with glucose and oxygen. If you are doing a lot of endurance work the capillaries will actually grow, like new twigs sprouting from a branch.

Inside the muscle fibres, equally important changes take place. The chemical reactions by which the fuel is broken down and converted into energy are carried out by enzymes. With more training, the muscle cells manufacture more enzymes, and so the muscle can produce more energy per minute. It also becomes more efficient at extracting oxygen from the bloodstream.

The energy is released in small 'packets' by a series of chemical reactions, but, with thousands of fibres involved, it appears to be continuously available. Glucose is broken down in several steps to pyruvic acid. If oxygen is available, the pyruvic acid is then broken down into carbon dioxide and water, with the release of energy. This is the 'aerobic' pathway. If energy is required very quickly, the pryuvic acid is converted directly into lactic acid. Since this does not require oxygen, it is known as the 'anaerobic' pathway. In both cases, the release of energy enables the muscle fibres to contract, and so your legs move.

It has recently been discovered that muscle fibres are not all of the same type. There are at least three different types. The 'slow twitch' fibres work entirely by aerobic methods. Even if all the slow twitch fibres in a muscle are working at the same time, they cannot move the limbs as fast as the 'fast twitch' fibres, but they can go on almost indefinitely if they are supplied with fuel and oxygen.

The fast twitch fibres may get their energy by lactic acid production (fast twitch glycolytic) or by aerobic methods (fast twitch oxidative). They can cause the muscle to contract more quickly, but they cannot keep going for very long, because the accumulation of fatigue products, mostly lactic acid, poisons the muscle. Lactic acid is gradually got rid of. It is oxidized away, and the oxidation of part of it produces enough energy to convert the rest of it back to glucose. The amount of oxygen used for this process is known as the 'oxygen debt'. At the end of a flat-out sprint, you will have accumulated the maximum oxygen debt. It is the accumulation of lactic acid in the muscles which is the chief cause of fatigue in a middle distance race.

The proportion of fast twitch and slow twitch fibres in a particular muscle appears to be an inherited factor. You can, by specific training, develop one type of fibre more than another, but you cannot alter the proportion of the fibres. Alberto Salazar's muscles are ninety per cent of the slow twitch type whereas Sebastian Coe's muscles are about fifty per cent fast twitch and fifty per cent slow twitch. If you are predominantly a 'slow twitch' person you will never be able to sprint very fast and, conversely, the fast twitch person will not be able to run a good marathon because he lacks the fibres which can use oxygen and produce energy without a lot of fatigue products accumulating.

The sprinter is like a drag-racing car. He has a big heavy engine which burns up fuel very quickly and uneconomically but it goes very fast. The long distance runner is like a fuel economy car: it doesn't go very fast, but it uses up fuel very slowly and there is not too much wear and tear on its parts, so they last a long time. The middle distance runner, and this includes the 5000m runner as well, is more like a rally car. He must be able to run efficiently for a long time without burning up all his fuel, but at times he must use additional power, relying on anaerobic resources, to produce maximum speed over short stretches, usually near the finish.

If two runners are the same height and weight, with the same maximum oxygen intake, they may still be of quite different abilities. The one with more fast twitch fibres will outsprint the other, but the one with more slow twitch fibres will probably have a steady pace closer to maximum oxygen intake. Physical build introduces another variable. If a runner has short legs, he may be able to move them very fast, and so be an efficient sprinter, but this will be wasteful of energy. The 400m/800m runner traditionally has long legs *and* can move them quite fast. This gives him the necessary speed for his distance, but is too wasteful of energy to be effective at distances longer than one mile at the most.

For the long distance runner, economy of effort is what matters. Some have a long stride, some a shorter one, but it is usual to find that, as a distance runner becomes more efficient, his stride length decreases. A long 'floating' stride has its drawbacks, because it is only when your foot is in contact with the ground that you are able to push yourself forwards.

There are other abilities peculiar to the marathon runner. If ability depended entirely on the fibres and their oxygen intake we would be able to assess someone's potential by a 10-minute test on a treadmill, but this cannot, thank goodness, be done. A man with the right build and an economical style may at any given speed be using ten per cent less fuel and oxygen than an ungainly runner of the same weight.

Let us go back to our man jogging. If he is going at a very gentle jog, 6 miles per hour, he is burning up about 600 kilocalories (kcal) an hour. If his fat reserves are releasing available energy, in the form of 'free fatty acids', at a rate of, say, 400kcal an hour, he will only be using up his glycogen reserves at a rate of 200kcal an hour. If we assume these reserves to total between 1000 and 1500kcal, he should be able to manage the marathon distance easily, with plenty of glycogen in reserve.

If he speeds up to 9 miles per hour, a speed of 6 minutes 40 seconds per mile, he will be using up energy at a rate of 900kcal an hour. He is likely to run into difficulties for three distinct reasons. First of all, if we assume that he is still getting 400kcal an hour from his fat reserves, which

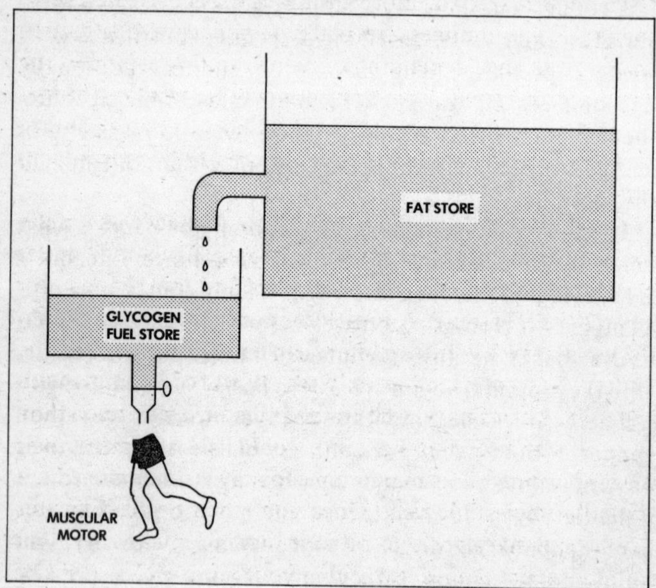

may or may not be the case, he is running down his glycogen reserves at a rate of 500kcal an hour. If his total glycogen reserve is only 1200kcal, he is going to exhaust that in less than 2 hours 30 minutes, by which time he will only have completed 22 miles. He will hit the wall. When the glycogen reserves get very low, the body operates a sort of 'safety shut-down' procedure, so that all you can draw on is your energy from fat and protein, plus a trickle from glycogen stores.

The picture opposite may make it clearer to you. When he has exhausted most of his glycogen stores, energy is still available, but only enough for him to move at 4 or 5 miles per hour. Our man is reduced to the sort of shambling walk-jog that we see in the last stages of a race. Of course, if he has the sense to realize what is going on, he will slow his pace before he runs smack into the wall.

There is a second, more insidious aspect to the use of energy. Some muscles are better supplied with glycogen than others and, depending on your running style and the nature of the going, some muscles will be working harder than others. There may be a local shortage of glycogen. This could affect someone running on a hilly course, who has not been training on hills.

The third source of danger may lie in the fact that 9 miles per hour is just too fast for some people. Covering 9 miles per hour means using up about 50ml of oxygen per kilogram per minute. A top-class runner, whose maximum oxygen intake is 75ml/kg/min., can manage the pace easily, because he is working at only two-thirds of his maximum capacity. An ordinary, well-trained person, with a maximum oxygen intake of 55ml/kg/min., would have to work at over ninety per cent of his maximum capacity to maintain this, a virtually impossible task. Once you reach a speed greater than about sixty per cent of your maximum capacity, you start to accumulate lactic acid in your leg muscles. A really efficient marathon runner will be able to run at closer to his maximum speed than others, maybe at eighty-five per cent, but everyone has a limit. As the lactic acid accumulates in your muscles, you get a feeling of tiredness and eventually you are forced to slow down.

Most of us cannot have the testing done which tells us what our maximum oxygen intake is, or what our fuel reserves are, but we find these things out by trial and error. If you run in a mile race, flat out, you finish up exhausted and out of breath. You have acquired an oxygen debt, because you have burned up your glucose at a very fast rate. You have not had time to take in all the oxygen you need. Lactic acid has accumulated, and you need to go on breathing hard for a few minutes to make up the oxygen debt. Your one-mile time is run at a speed which represents about 120 per cent of your maximum oxygen intake. It is not a very good guide to your marathon potential, because a good miler can tolerate more lactic acid and usually has more sheer muscle power. A better guide to your oxygen intake capacity is the time you take for a race or time-trial of 2 to 3 miles. If you can run this at, say, 6 minutes per mile, you can take this as representing 100 per cent of your oxygen intake capacity.

If you run in a 6-mile race you should be able to run at about ninety per cent of your maximum capacity, so our 6-minute miler should be able to maintain around 6 minutes 40 seconds per mile. His marathon speed will probably be about seventy-five per cent of his maximum capacity, which means about 7.5 miles per hour, or 8 minutes per mile.

This gives you a rough idea about what sort of pace you should be able to maintain, but whether you *can* maintain it depends, of course, on your carbohydrate reserves – your glycogen stores. In the 1982 Philadelphia Marathon I set myself a pace of 5 minutes 45 seconds per mile. I was a little slower than this at the 10-mile point, but, feeling pretty good, I increased my pace and with the help of some downhill running I managed to run the next 10 miles in 56 minutes. By the time I reached 19 miles I was feeling weak, and by the time I reached the feeding station at 20 miles I knew that I really had drained away my energy reserves. The last 6 miles were run at 7-minute mile speed. Although my oxygen intake system, heart, lungs and blood vessels, could handle 5 minutes 45 seconds per mile or even 5 minutes 30 seconds, I hadn't got the carbohydrate reserves to go the full distance.

A few months later I ran another marathon, in which my concern was merely to finish the course at a steady speed. I ran 7-minute miles for the first 10 miles, and 6 minute 45 miles for the next 10. The wall I had feared was no longer there. I found that I could increase the speed quite easily, and finished the last 6 miles at just over 6-minute mile speed. What was different from my experience in Philadelphia? For one thing, I was running down my fuel reserves much more slowly, at around 400 to 500kcal an hour instead of nearly 700kcal an hour. Second, the steady running I had done in training in the preceding three months had increased my carbohydrate reserve.

You may ask why it is that we get tired at all when going very slowly. If there are unlimited supplies of fat for energy, and an unlimited supply of oxygen, why can't we continue at a slow pace for ever, supplementing our fat reserves by drinking glucose as we run? There are other aspects to fatigue. One is neuro-muscular. The connection between a muscle and the nerve which tells it what to do is a chemical one, and after prolonged use the supplies of the chemical messenger may run down and the rate of transmission of the command may decrease. Another aspect is hormonal. The release of fuels for respiration is under the control of hormones, which are produced by the endocrine glands, under the control of the 'master gland', the pituitary. Supplies of hormones from the pituitary and other glands may run low. I have a suspicion that this is the reason why we cannot run many good 10,000m or marathon races in a short space of time, because of the regeneration needed in the endocrine glands, but this is not proven.

Finally, any system is only as strong as its weakest point. If some particular muscles are low in glycogen, they may tire, throwing more strain on to another muscle. If this is already working as hard as it can, the extra strain may cause fibres to tear, or it may release fluid, causing the muscle to stiffen up.

Very often, the whole system will slow down, due to overheating and dehydration. If the fluid lost by sweating is more than two per cent of the total weight, muscular efficiency starts to fall off. The loss of electrolytes (salts) may cause muscular cramp. At very high temperatures, the brain is affected, and in a long race the winner is often the person who can best control or tolerate the rise in body temperature. The longer the race, the more true it is that the race is not to the swiftest but to thc toughest. This means that the ambitious runner must develop every facet of his ability, correcting his weak points and building on his strong points.

What training does for you

It is generally true to say that the more specific the training is to your event, the more likely it is to do you good. Coaches and athletes have always known this instinctively, and over the years they have done the right things for the wrong reasons. However, it is impossible for the would-be 4-minute miler to keep on running quarter-miles in 60 seconds each all day long. Now that we know at least something of what is going on, we can work on one thing at a time.

Speed. We can develop the fast twitch fibres by doing anaerobic training and making those fibres work very hard. Weight training will increase the size of the fibres, and such things as hill training and resistance running will produce a similar effect, using the bodyweight as resistance. Since the middle distance runner needs an oxygen supply as well as strong muscles, I feel that the hill training or the low weight, many-repetitions type of training is of more use. Some great middle distance runners have used weights a lot, others have not touched them. There is very little evidence that weight training does anything for long distance runners at all, and since most of us need all the time available to get the miles in, time spent on weight training would seem to be unproductive. The only exception is in times of injury, when muscle strength can be maintained, and weak muscles restored, by specific weight training exercises.

The ability to sprint fast at the end of a distance race does not depend solely on muscle strength. It is partly a skill which can be learned and must be practised. It is very easy for the distance runner, lacking in fast twitch fibres, to say 'I haven't got any speed' and therefore neglect speed training. The technique of running fast is best practised when you are fresh. The runner who is used to running economically has got to change his style. He has got to pick his knees up, drive with his arms, get up on his toes, and at the same time he has to think about running as straight as possible and as smoothly as possible.

Fast runs are included in many sessions at the end of a long run. This is because, having learned to sprint, the distance runner has to get used to running fast when he is tired. This factor will also come in at the end of hard interval and repetition sessions. The skilled runner, going flat out at the end of a race, still looks smooth and relaxed even when he is close to exhaustion, because he has practised the movements over and over again.

Flexibility. This quality is important to the middle distance runner in particular. When running fast, muscles are alternately contracted and relaxed several times a second. If there is a slight shortening of one muscle, particularly around the hip or thigh region, this muscle will cause resistance during one phase of the stride. This will either shorten the stride, so that you do not go as far with a given amount of effort, or else it will require more effort to maintain stride length.

Sebastian Coe is held up as an example of the perfect running style for middle distance. Although he is not very tall – only 5 feet 9 inches – he manages to maintain a good stride length as well as a high rate of striking. This is partly attributable to the attention he pays to flexibility. His winter training mileage is not great – no more than 50 miles a week – but he does have several regular gymnasium sessions a week. A typical set of exercises would go as follows:

Flexibility exercises

1 Achilles tendon stretch. Stand, facing a wall, with one foot a short pace in front of the other. Lean forwards, keeping both heels flat on the ground, and your arms supporting you on the wall.

2 Calf stretch. As for the first exercise, but allowing your heels to come off the ground.

3 Hamstring stretch. Stand on one leg, with the other leg out in front of you, resting on a beam or a table, about three feet off the ground. Lean forward without bending the knees.

4 Gluteal stretch. Standing on your right leg, lift your left knee up towards your chin. Use both hands to grasp the left knee and pull it upwards. Repeat with the other leg.

5 Quadriceps stretch. Standing on your left leg, grasp your right ankle with your right hand. Pull the leg up and back underneath the body. Repeat with the other leg.

6 Lower back stretch. Lie on your front and raise your head and chest up off the ground.

7 Hip stretch. Lying on your front, raise one leg

upwards and backwards. The stretch can be increased by getting a partner to pull the leg, *gently*, further backwards.

In all the above exercises, the stretch should be taken to the point of mild discomfort and held there for 30 seconds. At the end of this time you should find that you can briefly stretch a little further before relaxing. Repeat each exercise at least twice, which means about twenty minutes for the full set.

Strength training

The following set of exercises, using the body's own weight as resistance, can be done as a circuit, indoors or outdoors. Although they will not develop as much strength as using weights, they will improve both the strength and endurance of the muscles used for propulsion and support.

1 Sit-ups. Keep the feet still and keep your hands behind your head. Move gradually from a prone to a sitting position and back again.

2 Press-ups. These can be made harder by having your feet on a chair or bench, higher than the rest of the body.

3 Squat thrusts. Start in the press-up position and bring your knees forwards quickly, under your chest, then shoot your legs back again.

4 Low thrusts. Starting from the sprint start position, spring high into the air, bring the back leg through, so that you land in the start position again, with the legs reversed.

5 Depth jumps. Bouncing over a series of low (1–2 feet) obstacles, either on one leg or with both legs together.

6 Beam jumps. Supporting yourself on a beam, 4–5 feet off the ground, drop to the ground and spring up again.

7 Leg raising. Lying on your back, or hanging on wall bars, raise your legs and slowly lower them.

8 Trunk raising. Lie across a stool, with your feet braced against wall bars but with your trunk supported. Raise your head and shoulders as far as possible and lower again.

Most of these exercises are found in all circuit training,

but exercises 4, 5 and 6, which are used by George Gandy in his Loughborough gym circuit, are particularly useful for runners.

The number to be done here is infinitely variable, but as a rough guide, try doing each exercise ten times per circuit, and go round the circuit three times in a training session, and do this twice a week in addition to your running. Once it comes easily, increase the number of reps in each exercise.

Anaerobic capacity. This refers to the distance you can run at your maximum speed. The greater your anaerobic capacity, the longer you will be able to maintain your finishing speed in a race. The types of training session which will develop this are:

1 Long hills. Running fast up a long hill, 120 to 400m long, until you can feel your legs going rubbery, and then doing it again

2 Long sprints, e.g., repeat 300m runs on the track, at a speed close to that of your best 400m

3 Repetition runs over 500m/600m, at your 800m speed

4 The last few runs in an interval session, e.g., 12 × 400m with a 2 minute recovery, if they are done fast

5 Running fast over sand dunes or similar going.

Aerobic capacity. Improving your ability to take in oxygen will enable you to have a faster 'steady state'. You may be able to run for several miles at a speed of 5 minutes 30 seconds per mile, but to be a really good distance runner you have to be able to run at 5-minute mile speed without getting into oxygen debt. The necessary improvements in your heart capacity, the development of the muscle capillaries and the enzymes in your muscle fibres will come from the following types of session:

1 Steady running with your pulse rate in the 145 to 165 range, e.g., a brisk 6 to 8 mile run

2 Interval or Fartlek running, where your pulse rate is repeatedly raised to close to 180 and kept there for over 30 seconds at a time. After a short interval, in which the pulse rate drops to below 120, another effort is made, e.g., a typical session might be 15 to 20 × 400m in 67 seconds, with 1 minute 30 seconds recovery jog

3 Repetition running, e.g., 6 × 1200m. This combines features of sessions 1 and 2, and closely simulates racing conditions.

You do not have to run flat out to get this aerobic benefit. If you do too much flat-out training, you are working anaerobically. Development of aerobic capacity takes time, and a lot of the training will be done at an effort level which is only 'fairly hard', about two-thirds of maximum effort.

General endurance and heat tolerance. Both these aspects will be improved simply by increasing the number of miles you run per week. They will be improved still further by increasing the length of your longest run. Heat tolerance can be improved by doing more training in warm weather or by wearing more clothing, e.g., an extra sweat shirt, when training in normal temperatures. The speed is not very important, as long as you do not walk, so you can develop these factors when too tired to work on others.

Fuel reserve. This is very important to marathon runners, but unimportant to people running distances of less than a half-marathon. It will develop gradually as you increase the number of miles you run per week, but the best way of improving it is to put in a really long run on an empty stomach, e.g., 15 to 20 miles after work. This will cause the body to store up more glycogen, and also stimulate the breakdown of fatty acids and their release into the bloodstream. In the short term you can improve fuel supply by taking glucose drinks during the race or by going on the marathon diet (see Chapter 12).

6

The Road Runner

Since this is the route by which the majority of runners come into the sport, there is little need for me to point out the benefits of road running. You can get a race almost every weekend in all parts of the country, and since there are so many people taking part, you can always find someone of your own standard to run with or against. Unlike cross-country, the road surface is the same all the year round, so you can compare training and racing times from year to year, and you can compare times over standard distances, such as the 10km, between one country and other. Though it may sometimes be unpalatable, road running tells you the truth about yourself.

The only drawback is that it is a hard surface, and for beginners, particularly, the jarring effect may cause pain in knees and ankles. It doesn't have to; there are plenty of marathon runners putting in 120 miles a week on the road, year in and year out, without injury, but you have got to be careful when you start. If you skipped Chapter 3, go back and note my suggestion about alternating between hard and soft surfaces during the first few weeks of training, and take care in choosing the right shoes (also Chapter 3). Even when you feel that you have got used to regular road work, and it is the most convenient surface on which to run, make an effort to run on a soft surface at least once a week.

Let me assume that you have got over those early stages and have been trying out the Jogger-into-Runner schedule in Chapter 4, doing about 30 miles a week. You now decide that you are going to concentrate on road running for the next six months, without going up to the longer distances –

half-marathon and above – except as an occasional experiment. You want to run as effectively as you can in road races from 5 to 10 miles, and you may find yourself running a 3-mile stage in a road relay. All these events come into the same bracket, because they are almost entirely aerobic events, and although endurance is required, it is not the same type of endurance that is needed for a marathon. What you need to develop is the ability to run fast, with an economical style, and at the same time you must build up the special muscular endurance to last out a 10-mile race.

The right kind of mileage for these events is between 40 and 60 miles a week. With less than 40, you may be able to do high quality training but you won't reach your full potential over 10 miles. With more than 60 miles, a lot of your work is likely to be too slow. Of course, this is for the average runner. The man or woman who is aiming for international level may be up to 70 or 80 miles a week, though personally I don't believe that this is essential. There are two schools of thought about mileage, or perhaps two temperamental types. There are the people who don't like putting themselves under pressure, but who are quite prepared to run long distances at an easy pace; and there are those who feel that training can't be doing them any good unless they push themselves hard. I've been in running long enough to realize that each type has something to learn from the other. I used to belong to the 'high-pressure' school, probably because I was desperately ambitious and I didn't want to waste any time. As I got older I realized that the longer, slower runs were enjoyable and could be fitted into any programme without lowering my ability to run fast. It was brought home to me by seeing the New Zealander, Peter Snell, a Lydiard-trained man, going out and running 20 miles during the week between breaking the world mile record and the world 800m record.

On the other side of the coin, I have come across a huge number of people who have been led to believe that training just means running a set number of miles at the same, rather slow pace. Once I introduced them to some of my methods of quality training they found the running more interesting *and* they found their racing speed improving considerably.

Until you find the pattern that suits you best, I suggest that you start with steady running, up to your selected mileage, let us say 50 miles a week. As you are aiming to race at 10 miles you will have one long slow run a week at least, say 10 to 13 miles, and with one rest day you will be doing 7 or 8 miles on the other five days. I don't recommend twice a day training at this level – you are much better off doing one run a day properly. Of the five days, one should be over a short course, 5 or 6 miles. This means that on the other days you will be training about one hour a day, and you should be alternating easy days and harder days. If you plod along at the same pace, you are not going to improve beyond a certain point. The only way you get better is by pushing yourself just that little bit harder. The right sort of level is something approaching your 6-mile racing speed – maybe 15 seconds per mile slower – in your hard runs, while in the easy runs there should be no sense of pressure and the speed may be a minute a mile slower. There are many different systems in operation in your body and each type of training will bring improvement in different ways.

Your pattern for the first six or eight weeks will therefore look like this:

Schedule 4. Daily Training for the Road Racer

Sunday: Long slow run, 10 to 13 miles
Monday: 7 to 8 miles easy pace, but putting in bursts up the hills

Tuesday: The hardest day. 1 to 2 miles jogging, then timed run over a 3-mile course, then 1 mile jogging
Wednesday: On grass or paths. 7 to 8 miles easy running
Thursday: Brisk run round 5 to 6 mile course
Friday: Rest
Saturday: Race. If no race try to do something strenuous but different

When you have had some racing experience you will feel that you need to build up your weak points, of which sustained running speed is the most important. I have found that the most effective way of doing this is the road repetition run, over a distance long enough to get a lot of training effect, but short enough for you to operate at racing speed. This means a distance that takes you between 3 minutes and 7 minutes to run. A mile is a good distance, though it doesn't have to be an exact mile. You are going to be running these at the speed you would run in a 5- or 6-mile race, so they will be quite tiring. The recovery time should be no longer than the time for the run, and once you have fixed your recovery time, stick to it for the whole session, so that you can make valid comparisons week by week.

How many miles should you do? If you are aiming at racing 10km ($6\frac{1}{4}$ miles) then you should eventually be doing 6 miles of fast work, which means 6×1 mile – a hard session, and quite a lengthy one. I suggest that you start off with a total of 20 minutes of fast work and when you have got used to that, after three or four weeks, add one more repetition. The fast run should be preceded by the usual warm-up and stretching. During the recovery period, put on a sweat shirt or something to keep you warm, and walk about gently. I used to do these repetition runs round a circuit in our village, starting and finishing on my front doorstep. If the weather was bad I used to go inside for the rest period, but I found that it was very hard to get out again for the next effort.

The next factor which most people will want to improve is their absolute speed. The question I get asked is: 'I have plenty of stamina, but I just can't run fast; what should I do?' In most cases it is a meaningless question, because it is probably not speed that matters, but fitness, and as you get fitter, you will run faster over your courses. However, there are times when you need speed in some form – for example, if you are asked to run in a road relay, over a short distance, say 2 or 3 miles, which demands a much faster tempo than you are used to. If you have taken up running again after a long break, you may have lost the skill of fast running which comes naturally to most teenagers.

If you think about it, running fast makes quite different demands on your muscular system. You have to increase your stride length, which means picking your knees up higher, getting up on to your toes at the end of each stride and getting more push from your ankles. At the same time your back muscles and abdominal muscles have to work harder to keep your upper body still, and you have to use a more vigorous arm action to keep yourself balanced. As you will be running at your maximum oxygen intake, your chest muscles have to work harder too. I find that when I am running at a steady speed, I complete a full breathing cycle every four strides, but when I am running fast I complete it every two strides.

The acquisition of speed should start by putting in short 10-second bursts during your easy runs. Start on the flat, or slightly uphill, increase your rate of striding first, then speed up still more by picking your knees up and consciously driving with your arms. Think of throwing your hands downwards on each stride. The first few times, all you should do is accelerate up to your maximum speed, hold it for ten strides and then ease gradually down again. Don't brake hard to slow yourself down, just 'freewheel' until your speed comes back to a jog.

Increasing your stride length puts more strain on your hamstring muscles. If you are trying to increase speed you must do your stretching exercises conscientiously before you start training. For more advice on speed work, see Chapter 9.

The ability to run fast depends on your leg muscle power, which is what most people mean by the term 'strength'. If you can increase this, you will also tire less quickly at any given speed. However, pure strength alone will not meet the needs of the distance runner, otherwise you would find that weightlifters would be the best distance runners. What you need is the combination of strong muscles with the transport system to supply those muscles with fuel and oxygen. It is no good just doing weight training, and it is no good just doing flat-out sprinting, because what you need are muscles that have the speed *and* the endurance. The next step from doing short bursts is to move to a session in which developing your speed is the main thing, though with a certain amount of endurance effect. Since too much running at speed leads to a build-up of lactic acid in the muscle, it is best to intersperse the speed work with periods of steady running. If you have a nice area of grass, a firm path or a stretch of beach to use, arrange things so that you have a couple of miles of easy running on the way there, then put in a speed session – say ten runs of 150 yards each, working up to a fast striding speed, which is just short of a flat-out sprint. The recovery period here should be *at least* twice as long as the run; after getting your breath back, walk or jog slowly for the same distance as the run, which may mean just going back to the start, if it's a small area.

How much speed training is enough? When you get tired,

your speed will fall off and you will find it difficult to maintain your stride length. That is the time to stop. When you get really fit, you will be able to have a 15-minute jog and then come back for another session, thus combining both speed and endurance. I find that this is mentally a very easy session to do, and when I was running at my peak I regularly used to do a session of three sets of 10 × 200m, with a 5-minute jog between sets.

The best ways of building strength and speed are through using hills, because you are using your body weight as a form of weight training, and you are in a running situation. I have gone into typical hill training for winter in the cross-country chapter (Chapter 8), and into speed work for milers in Chapter 9. The road runner has the advantage that he is coming across hills during every training session, and if you get into the habit of making an effort every time you meet a hill, you will get more value from your runs.

When you have learned to incorporate these types of training into your week, you will be getting a lot more useful training done without much increase in either the mileage or the time taken. The pattern of hard days on Tuesday and Thursday, with a race on Saturday, can be followed unless it is a really important race, in which case you do your hard training on the preceding Monday and Wednesday, giving yourself two easy days. The pattern will now look like this:

Schedule 5. Two-Week Programme Before a 10km Race

WEEK 1

Sunday: 10 to 12 miles easy

Monday: 2-mile jog, two sets of 8 × 150m on grass, 2-mile jog

Tuesday: Warm-up, then 5 × 1¼ mile circuit, timed. (6 minutes rest)

Wednesday: Steady 7 to 8 miles, preferably off the road

Thursday: Brisk 6 miles, with bursts up hills
Friday: Rest
Saturday: Minor race, plus 4 to 5 miles running about before and after

WEEK 2
Sunday: 12 to 14 miles easy
Monday: Brisk 8 miles, including 8 to 10 × 300m fast bursts
Tuesday: 6 miles on grass, easy running plus strides
Wednesday: 2-mile jog, then 2 miles, untimed, at fast speed. Five minutes rest, then one timed lap of the 1¼ mile circuit
Thursday: 3 to 5 miles easy
Friday: Rest or 3-mile jog
Saturday: Race

Progression

The biggest problem that the British road runner has to face is having too many races. He may be asked by his club to run in relays or team road races; he will have some local events which he would like to take part in; he will probably want to try one or two long races during the year; and he may be tempted to go to some exciting overseas event, or to run in the county cross-country. All this is a lot of fun, but it can be destructive. Races will help you get better as long as you give yourself enough rest after them, and as long as you don't go in for races for which you are not properly prepared. If you do get dragged into some event you are not ready for, try to treat it as training. For example, if you are entered in a 10-mile race and you feel that you haven't had the time to get ready for it, don't take the approach of 'blast out and hang on', but take the first 3 or 4 miles at a deliberately comfortable speed and then try to run a good last 6 miles.

In each year there should be one or more periods when you are really going out to get the best possible results. During this period, it is the races which count, not the training, and you have got to make sure that you have rested up enough *before* the race, and that you are fully recovered from it afterwards before starting hard training again. The two months leading up to this competitive season are the really important ones. This is where you should be training on the lines I have just suggested. In the rest of the year you should have a relaxation phase, a build-up phase and a maintenance phase.

Relaxation phase. You can stay pretty fit by jogging for half an hour three times a week, as long as you don't put on a lot of weight. Some people like to have a complete break, and it's a good idea. You can become so intense about your running that it ceases to be fun, and if you never have a break you never give your body a chance of getting rid of the niggling problems which often come from over-use. Quite apart from that, you can become a very boring and obsessional person if you never vary your routine. I suggest that you will do yourself more good than harm to have a couple of weeks – preferably in the summer – of doing nothing at all in the way of running, and another couple of weeks when you just go out for 20 or 30 minutes three times a week. You should come back from that refreshed and enthusiastic for the next phase.

Build-up phase. Here you are trying to get up to the weekly mileage you are aiming for in the main training period. It doesn't matter how you get the miles in at first, as long as you do them. You can even count walking, to start with. When you have reached your target, say 40 miles, by gradual increase, allow yourself an easy week before repeating the 40. As a general rule, it is a good thing to have one week in the month of lower mileage; this will normally come before your main races. The pattern for the 40-miles-a-week runner would be:

Schedule 6. Four-Week Programme for the 40-Miles-a-Week Runner

Week 1: 35 to 40 miles
Week 2: 40 to 45 miles
Week 3: 45 miles
Week 4: 35 miles

When you have done two consecutive weeks at your target mileage, start increasing the quality as suggested earlier. A variation on this is to make the target of your build-up period some long race, a half-marathon or more, so that you are doing a longer, slower type of training. When you switch over to your serious training, the distances will seem less daunting and you will be able to tackle them with confidence. I tried this with a lot of success when I was moving up to running 10km races; I made the Finchley 20 the object of my build-up phase, so that when it came to the choice between the short fast session or the long slow one, I chose the latter. Once I had the '20' behind me, the training necessary for 10km seemed easy.

Maintenance phase. This is for when you have reached a good state of fitness, but you cannot afford to put in the effort needed to go on moving up. How much do you need to stay racing fit? I would say that you must go out at least three times a week, and those minimum three days should be:

Schedule 7. The Maintenance Programme

Day 1: The long run – at least 9 miles
Day 2: The hard run. Either a fast continuous 5 miles or 3 × 1 mile repetition

Day 3: The speed session, either 10 × 300m, or 15 to 20 × 150m, done at a fast stride

If you have a race, this will do instead of day 2 or day 3. This is the very minimum you can get away with. If you lead a very sedentary life it may not be enough, but if your normal day includes quite a lot of walking about, physical work, or running up and down stairs, these three days will keep you racing fit. The other kind of maintenance phase is when you are on a fairly low level of fitness, not racing, but just aiming to stay fit enough to move into proper training when time allows. I would put this at around 20 miles a week, done in four sessions at a steady speed. From this you can go on to either cross-country, track or road schedules.

Road racing tactics

Everybody should run in a race. You never find out what you can do if you don't race. The day has gone when nobody ran in a race unless he or she was good. In the average local road race you will find men and women of all ages and degrees of fitness. That is what is so nice about the sport. You could not go in for a tennis tournament if you were a real beginner, but you can enter a race.

Remember that the race is really against yourself. It is nice to win prizes, age-group awards, team trophies and so on, but it only means something in relation to your own ability.

The guiding principle should be to run as close to level pace as possible. If you are hoping to run 10 miles in the hour, it is better to run the first mile in 6 minutes and then to move to level miles in the 5 minutes 55 seconds to 6 minute range, than to run 5 minutes 35 seconds for the first mile and then slow down. You may have gain 25 seconds on your schedule, but you will pay for it later on.

There will be some exceptions to level pace. On the hills you are going to be making a 6 minutes per mile effort, if we stick to the same example, but this will mean a 6 minute 15 seconds mile on a steady (five per cent) up-grade and a 5 minute 55 seconds mile on a down-grade. Unfortunately, you do not gain as much benefit on the downhill as you lose on the uphill, so hilly courses will always give you slower times than flat courses. Because hills are tough, they are usually crucial in race tactics.

How to run hills. In training, you always get used to making an effort up the hill, because it is good training. By using your body weight as resistance and really driving up the hills, you get a lot of benefit in leg strength. Probably for this reason, a lot of runners drive hard up the hills in a race. This is a mistake, because the consciously hard driving action, with a correspondingly long stride, is wasteful of energy. You will have to make more effort on a hill in order to prevent your speed from dropping, or merely to stay in touch with your rivals, but it is more economical to speed up by taking a shorter stride. If you lean forwards slightly, shorten your stride and work your arms a little more, you will glide up the hills with only a little more effort than running on the flat. If you want to break away from the group you are with, the time to do it is over the top of the hill, while the others are relaxing from the effort of the climb. If you can summon up the strength, you should increase your stride length just as the hill starts to flatten out, and stride away over the brow of the hill. You will feel tired, but you can get your breath back as you run down the other side, and you may gain those vital few yards and lose contact with those who are still struggling up the hill.

Breaking away. If you are running a race, as opposed to a mere time-trial, you are going to take a gamble at some stage, to give yourself a chance of really doing well, even of winning. This gamble may take the form of setting out at a faster level pace than you have ever run before, say 5 minutes 30 seconds per mile for the person who normally runs 6-minute miles. More likely, you will set off at your normal pace, which is as fast as you can comfortably maintain, and keep this going until you approach the halfway point, where you, and the others around you, are starting to slow down. Now somebody has to make a decision. If you are feeling confident you will try to pick up the pace and break away. If you do this it has got to be decisive, with a sharp increase in pace, even if it is only temporary. It is no good coming up on the shoulder of the leader and gradually moving past him.

Running races involves bluffing. You have got to convince your opponents that you are better than they are. When you move past someone, try to run tall, look easy and move past fast, keeping the increased pace going until you have got at least 10 yards clear of him, preferably 20 yards. When you have gone past, try to relax as much as possible without dropping the pace, and don't look round. Your ears will tell you whether or not your break has succeeded.

Closing the gap. You find yourself the pace-setter for your group, and you are running along quite happily when someone comes past you and makes a break. What do you do? You don't panic and you don't give up. There are two possibilities – either he is better than you or he is not. If he really is better, and has moved up to a different tempo, there is not much you can do about it, but if he is not better than you, his burst is probably only a bit of bluff. The effort of making the burst will have tired him, and if you watch him carefully, you will see that after a few seconds the gap between you does not get any bigger. This is the time to start reeling him in, gradually. Imagine that you are attached to the back of his shirt by a piece of elastic, which is gradually shortening.

If I am trying to close the gap on someone who is 100 yards or more ahead of me, I use a couple of devices. I note when he passes a corner or a road sign, and then I count in seconds until I reach that point myself. I then look ahead and note him passing another point, and try to reach it in a slightly shorter time. If the gap is a big one, I try putting my head down and running for fifty or 100 paces, counting the paces, until I raise my head and look for my opponent. In this way the closing of the gap becomes more perceptible.

Relaxing in a race. We all know how easy it is to run fast and relaxed. We see Steve Ovett doing it on television. He appears to lope along, holding himself back, and the commentator says: 'Rather a slow first lap, just on 60 seconds; Ovett will want something faster than this'. Then you go on to the track and try to run one lap in 60 seconds – it is a flat-out sprint for some, a total impossibility for most. How does he do it? For a start, he possesses the stride length and the muscle fibres to run fast; he could run a 50 seconds lap as a schoolboy. On top of that, however, the Ovetts, the Crams and the Salazars go out and practise running fast, day after day, over and over again, until they become very good at it. Running fast is a skill, a set of neuro-muscular responses which respond to training. Many ordinary runners do their training at a speed which is slower than their racing speed for 3 miles, or certainly no faster. If you want to be able to run a fast but relaxed mile on the road, you have got to condition yourself by running at that tempo at least once a week. This is why a road runner's schedule should include Fartlek and interval training. When doing a steady 8-mile run on the road, you can put in regular bursts of one minute's duration in which you are hitting a fast tempo. For the person who customarily runs 6-minute miles in a road race, I suggest that you try running quarter-miles (400m) in 80 seconds each, which is a 5 minute 20 second per mile speed. You will need to use a slightly different action, but the more you practise it, the easier it will become, and your cardiovascular development will take place along with the change of style, so that you will get the increased fitness to maintain the pace. You will have to give it time, two or three months, but it will happen.

Even in a slow race, it is possible to profit from knowing how to relax. You are in the middle stages of a 10-mile race, and running at about 6 minutes per mile. You are feeling a bit tired, but you know you cannot afford to slow down. Now is the time to find ways of saving energy. For a few strides, let everything drop, arms, hands, knees, shoulders, head, and run on your heels. Now bring each muscle into play gently, tensing it no more than is absolutely necessary to keep your speed going. Raise your head so that you are gazing at the road 50 yards in front of you. Swing your arms lightly, without tensing your neck and shoulder muscles, and try to use your wrists and hands to balance your leg action rather than your whole upper body. Does that feel easier? It should. Now for the really important part, the leg action. You are running with a short stride, landing on your heels. Try using your calf, ankle and foot slightly more, to lengthen your stride while keeping to the same tempo. This should increase your pace with little extra effort. Check your breathing. Are you breathing from the diaphragm? Is your breathing rhythm tied in to your striding rhythm? You should be completing a breathing cycle, a complete in and out, every four strides, except in the final sprint, when you will probably be breathing in and out every two strides. If you consciously monitor the use of every muscle, it is surprising how much energy you can save. I sometimes find that I am not using my feet fully, tending to run on the sides. In a long road race you will be less liable to injury if you can learn to push off with the whole of the front part of the foot, using every toe.

Timing your finish. The runner who comes tearing in at tremendous speed, near the back of the field, always gets a round of applause. I usually join in – we are supposed to be encouraging each other – but I usually say to myself, 'What an idiot!' and if it is one of my young athletes I go and talk to him afterwards. I say: 'That was a great finish, but if you felt as fresh as that, why didn't you run faster early on?' The true reason is either lack of confidence or else plain laziness.

If you are running a really good race, you will be getting more and more tired as you approach the finish, but yet your speed will not decrease; it may even increase as you use your anaerobic reserve. When you are warming up for a race, run over the last half-mile of the course at least, so that you know exactly where you are as you approach the finish line. It is impossible to maintain a finishing sprint for more than 200m at the end of a road race, and very often 100m is all you can manage, so make a note of the point where you can start by giving it all you have left. If there is a hill or a bend near the finish, it is often worth putting in a minor burst just as you pass that point, so that you can snatch a few yards' advantage before the run-in. The final point is to be sure to keep your place after you have passed the finish line and go into the finishing funnel. The person behind you may in a large field be shoved in front of you in the funnel, so that he or she is given your finishing place and time and you get theirs. After all the effort you have made to get there, it would be a shame not to receive your just reward.

7
The Marathon Runner

The marathon is a ridiculous distance. You don't have to run a marathon to prove that you are fit, and the time that you need to spend on training beforehand is bound to impinge upon normal life. The race itself takes for ever, and you feel dreadful afterwards. You feel tired for the next week. Why do we do it?

We do it because it *is* hard. To run 26 miles at any speed requires courage as well as fitness. For the modern man or woman it is probably the greatest physical challenge he or she will meet in life, and the challenge is there, in his or her own town. Circumstances prevent us from driving in the Le Mans 24-hour race, or playing at Wimbledon, or sailing the Atlantic single-handed, but the marathon is something which we can do, if we set our hearts and minds – and legs – to the task.

You've probably met the man in the pub who says: 'They're all running marathons these days, old women, little kids; there's nothing to it.' The short answer to him is: 'Let's see you try it, mate!' A lot of people *are* running marathons, but it is still the same distance, and it is just as hard to cover that distance as it ever was. The difference is that a time of, say, 2 hours 35 minutes, which before the war would have put you into the British team, will today win you a minor trophy in the over-forty category – if you're lucky.

Because of the very large number of competitors, and because many of the runners are going to take twice as long over the race as the winners, the whole attitude to the race is different. You don't see men running in track races who are hoping to beat 8 minutes for the mile. In a normal club race, on the track or in cross-country, there will be a lot of runners finishing within ten per cent of the winner's time. If it is a 5000m race, and the winner does 15 minutes, a lot of the field will finish under 16 minutes 30 seconds (within ten per cent) and everybody will finish under 18 minutes 45 seconds (within twenty-five per cent). If a marathon was won in 2 hours 24 minutes, the 'ten per cent' time would be 2 hours 38 minutes and the 'twenty-five per cent' time would be 3 hours exactly. The bulk of the field will be doing well if they beat the 'fifty per cent' time of 3 hours 36 minutes and some finishers will extend up to the '100 per cent' time of 4 hours 48 minutes.

The reasons for this are, first, that the marathon attracts a far wider spectrum of age and ability than the 'normal' racing distances, and, second, that most of the people taking part are a very long way from achieving their full potential, because they haven't done the right kind of training, or enough of it.

How much running do you need to do, and how long would it take to become a 'real' marathon runner? If you just want to finish, and if you have a sound background of either regular jogging or other sports training, you can follow the twelve-week plan below and have a good chance of finishing in somewhere between 3 and 4 hours. It is impossible to be dogmatic because so many people try the event, with so many different backgrounds. The first marathon I ran in, at the age of forty-two, took me 2 hours 50 minutes, on a basis of just over 30 miles a week, but I had maintained my fitness, and the same bodyweight, by staying in shape since I left school. Somebody who was 5 stones overweight would have very little chance of covering the distance even using the twelve-week plan.

The exercise physiologist, Dr Ron Maugham, himself a serious runner, did a breakdown of the results of the

Aberdeen Marathon, based on questionnaires filled in by the competitors. He found that there was a rough correlation between the number of miles a week done in training and the finishing time, but there were also spectacular exceptions. This is the reason for the controversy over weekly mileage. It *is* possible to run a marathon on 20 miles of training a week, but it is likely to be a slow marathon, and you are probably going to suffer. Nobody in the Aberdeen race ran a sub-2 hours 30 minutes without averaging over 40 miles a week for the previous two months, and nobody ran below 2 hours 20 minutes without averaging over 65 miles a week. Not surprisingly, most of the people running 70 miles or more per week were in the leading half of the race, and most of those averaging less than 30 miles a week were in the second half.

What does this tell us? First, we cannot be dogmatic about the right amount of mileage, because it is very much a matter of personal preference whether one is going to follow the LSD pattern (Long Slow Distance) or the low mileage, high intensity pattern. Secondly, don't believe the book which says: 'You *must* run 70 miles a week for the previous twelve weeks, if you want to run a marathon.' If you want to run one, go ahead and run it, and find out what it is like, but, believe me, it's going to be very tough in the last 6 miles!

The Marathon Hopeful plan

Let us suppose that in a drunken moment you have agreed to run a marathon in three months' time, and you have done no hard training at all, although you are basically quite fit and healthy, not overweight, and you have done some jogging. For this situation I have set out a Marathon Hopeful plan, as follows:

Schedule 8. The Marathon Hopeful Plan

Weeks to go	Weekly mileage	Composition of weekly training
12	20	3 × 4 miles; 1 × 8 miles
11	20–25	3 × 4 miles; 1 × 10 miles
10	25	3 × 5 miles; 1 × 10 miles
9	25–30	3 × 5 miles; 1 × 12 miles
8	30	2×5 miles; 1×8 miles; 1×12 miles
7	30	2×5 miles; 1×8 miles; 1×12 miles
6	30	2×5 miles; 1×6 miles; 1×14 miles
5	35	2 × 5 to 6 miles; 1 × 8 miles; 1 × 14 miles
4	40	2×6 miles; 1×10 miles; 1×16 miles
3	40	3 × 8 miles; 1 × 16 miles
2	35	3 × 7 miles; 1 × 14 miles
1	forget it!	1 × 12 to 14 miles on the Tuesday/ Wednesday, then gentle jogging

You can see that this schedule entails running four days a week, one day of which is a long one. You should not try to exceed this programme if you are a beginner, because the effects of increasing your running distance are cumulative, and you should not move up to 30 miles a week until you can cope with 25. Take the long-term view: the philosophy behind running is that you should enjoy life as much as poossible for as long as possible. Why risk injuring yourself by over-training, when you have so many years ahead of you? Remember the story of the old bull and the young bull? There were two bulls in a field, father and son, and they were separated from the herd of cows in the lower pasture by a big fence. One night there was a gale, which brought down a tree, which destroyed part of the fence. When the young bull saw this he became tremendously excited. 'Hey, dad, the fence is down. We can get at the cows. Let's run down there and do some of them! What do you say, dad? Shall we run down there and do some of them?' 'Certainly not,' said the old bull, 'we'll walk down there and do the whole lot.' For marathon runners, too, 'patience' is the watchword.

When you have run your first marathon, your first reaction will probably be 'never again', but after a few days you will begin to think: 'If only I'd been a bit fitter and done a bit more training, I could have done much better.' You only have to look at the way times have improved in the big marathons to see the truth of this. The woman who broke 4 hours the first time goes under 3 hours 30 minutes the next year, and the man who ran 3 hours 20 minutes is going for sub-3 hours, and so on down. As the Red Queen said to Alice: 'It takes all the running you can do to keep in the same place.'

If you have really been bitten by the bug, you may be asking, 'How soon can I run another?' I think that six weeks is about the ideal time between full marathons, because this will give you two weeks to recover from the first race, two weeks of your regular training cycle and two weeks of 'tapering' and mental preparation. I have gone into this later in the chapter, under the heading 'Strategy'. If you are the usual, rather weak-willed sort of person, it will probably be six months before you get around to another 26-miler, or possibly a year.

The twelve-week marathon preparation plan

Before embarking on this plan you should be following the ideas set out in Chapters 4 and 6, so you will be running 30 to 40 miles a week, with at least one session of quality training. You will have run in several road races in the previous year, including at least one marathon, so you will have some idea of what your expected marathon pace is, and you will know the difference between an easy 5 miles and a hard 5 miles.

Once again, I have made out a twelve-week plan because,

for most of us, life is too short and crowded to devote the entire year to building up for a particular race. This plan, based on my own experience, was published in *Running* magazine before the 1983 London Marathon. Quite a lot of people used it, and wrote in to say that it had worked well for them; I didn't receive any abusive letters from unsatisfied customers, so it has the seal of consumer approval. It is not, however, a perfect schedule, just a possible one. My ideas on the perfect schedule are not compatible with normal human existence.

Twelve weeks is long enough for you to be able to make the grade, if you can keep yourself at it. It does demand dedication during that time, but then, no one pretends that running a marathon is easy. The maximum weekly mileage is 60 miles, but we do not expect to attain that until weeks eight to ten and we taper off in the last two weeks leading up to the race.

In these twelve weeks, you may undergo some physical and mental changes: you are trying to go from the possible to the impossible – that is what training is about. You are trying to develop physical abilities which have lain dormant for years. You are trying to enlarge your physical scope in several different ways – in endurance, running speed and muscular strength – and above all you are trying to enlarge your mental scope to a point where you feel capable of tackling anything!

At this stage of the game, you have to take a tough line with yourself, which means less emphasis on the 'run for fun' element and more of the 'get out and do it' determination. I have therefore simplified the infinite number of types of training sessions to four important ones – the long run, the pace run, repetition runs and hill work.

The marathon is different from any other running event, in that it depends more on your endurance than on your ability to run at a certain speed. Any kid on the street can run a mile in 8 minutes, but he can't run 10 miles, let alone

26. The 30-miles-a-week runner can run a 10-mile race and can probably manage 15 at a push, but has no hope of maintaining his/her normal training speed over the marathon distance. The most important part of the schedule, therefore, is the long run, and this should *not* be skimped, whatever else may have to go. It does two things for you: first, it will train your whole body to increase its energy stores and, second, it will increase local muscular endurance.

In the time available, we can also make some improvement in two other factors – oxygen uptake and muscular strength. These are the factors which limit your normal running speed. We find that most marathon runners can run comfortably at about seventy to seventy-five per cent of their maximum oxygen uptake, so if you can improve your basic speed for a single mile, you will also improve your 'comfortable' speed. This can be seen by an improvement in your time in races or trials over the 5 to 10-mile distance. In training it can be gauged by the improvement in your times on 'repetition' circuits, of which more later.

The long run. There are only going to be eleven of these – the twelfth one will be the race itself. It does demand will power to go out on to the cold roads in the dark, so to make it easier, try to get a training companion and run it in daylight at the weekend. Make sure that you are properly clad, with a top that is wind- and rain-proof, and with a woolly hat and gloves. Getting *too* warm doesn't matter – it is good training for your temperature control system – but getting too cold just makes you miserable and can be dangerous.

If you haven't run long distances before in training (that is, 12 miles or more) it's a good idea to drive or cycle round the route first, so that you know where to expect the hills. You can also make a note of suitable toilet stops in case of emergency. You can then go into your long runs determined to finish, knowing that you have eliminated most of the possibilities which might hamper you. Every one which you succeed in doing will give you more confidence for the next one. You go like an Everest climber from base-camp to a higher camp and then on to another, until you are left with the final assault.

How fast should you go? On the slow side of comfortable, for the first one. Don't give yourself time targets, just make sure that you cover the distance, but do not walk. If you let yourself fall into the habit of walking, it ceases to be a continuous run and you lose much of the benefit.

The pace run. This will be a mid-week run, which means that it may be in the dark, so choose roads which are either traffic-free or which are well-lit, and wear reflective clothing. Run on the right, so that you are facing the traffic, unless there is a footpath you can use. The speed here is going to be a little faster than marathon speed, because you are only running for about 60 to 90 minutes. Mentally, this will proably be the hardest session of the week, because, unlike the long run, you must think about keeping your rhythm. It is advisable to start with a 1 to 2 mile warm-up, in full track suit and then strip down to what is comfortable for brisk running. This means that you need an 8 to 10 mile circuit from home. Do your stretching indoors first, then the warm-up run, then the circuit. Time yourself, and then finish off with whatever you need to complete the day's total mileage target.

The repetition run. This is another crucial part of all Tulloh training plans. It tests all the systems, because you are working at over ninety per cent of your maximum oxygen uptake, and you are keeping it up for at least a mile. I find that about a one-and-a-half mile circuit is best; if it is longer than that, it is difficult to keep up the pressure. The exact distance doesn't matter; what matters is improving your average time for a set of four to six repetitions, with a fixed time interval which should be about the same as the running time. In between the runs, put on your track suit, walk about and stretch gently. Your pulse rate should have dropped to a 'plateau' level of between 100 and 120 beats per minute before you start the next rep. Warm up with stretching and at least a mile of jogging before you start the session and jog for at least half a mile after the last one.

Hill runs. There is nothing to beat hills for increasing all-round strength. If you haven't run up and down hills in training, you will have all sorts of problems when you meet them in a race, because of the different muscles which are used. It doesn't matter whether you run round a hilly circuit or just run up and down the same hill, as long as you remember the words of the psalmist: 'I will lift up mine eyes unto the hills; from whence cometh my help?'

Schedule 9. Marathon Preparation Plan: Weeks 1 to 5

WEEK 1

Sunday: 6 miles easy
Monday: 8 miles; pace run – 6 miles, 2 miles warm up/down
Tuesday: 5 miles easy
Wednesday: 6 to 8 miles easy start, build up to fast finish
Thursday: 4 × 1½ miles, timed
Friday: Rest or 3 mile jog
Saturday: 10 miles easy
Total mileage: 41 to 46

WEEK 2

Sunday: 6 miles easy
Monday: 10 miles; pace run – 8 miles, as above
Tuesday: 5 miles easy
Wednesday: 6 to 8 miles easy start, build up to fast finish

Thursday: 6 miles hill run
Friday: Rest or 3 mile jog
Saturday: 12 miles easy
Total mileage: 45 to 50

WEEK 3
Sunday: 6 miles easy
Monday: 10 miles; pace run – 8 miles, as above
Tuesday: 5 miles easy
Wednesday: 6 to 8 miles easy start, build up to fast finish
Thursday: $4 \times 1\frac{1}{2}$ miles; aim to improve on average time
Friday: Rest or 3 mile jog
Saturday: 13 miles easy
Improve quality, rather than quantity
Total mileage: 46 to 51

WEEK 4
Sunday: 6 miles easy
Monday: 12 miles; pace run – 10 miles, as above
Tuesday: 5 miles easy
Wednesday: 6 to 8 miles easy start, build up to fast finish
Thursday: 6 miles hill run
Friday: Rest or 3 mile jog
Saturday: 13 miles easy
Total mileage: 48 to 53

WEEK 5
Sunday: 6 miles easy
Monday: 12 miles; pace run – 10 miles, as above
Tuesday: 5 miles easy
Wednesday: 6 to 8 miles easy start, build up to fast finish
Thursday: $4 \times 1\frac{1}{2}$ miles; aim to improve on average time
Friday: Rest or 3 mile jog
Saturday: 15 miles easy
Total mileage: 50 to 55

Five weeks of running between 45 and 55 miles a week, culminating in a 15-mile outing at the end of week 5, should have given you a good base for fitness, without extending you so much that you run into injury problems.

The next five weeks are the most important in your preparation for the big day, because the final two weeks will consist of 'tuning' sessions. In my experience, one's body takes at least a week, and sometimes two weeks, to get the benefit of a hard session, and so the work you put in weeks 9 and 10 will have the greatest effect on your state of fitness at the end of week 12.

There is an increase in the minimum volume of training to 55 and then to 60 miles a week during this period. This means an increase of fifty per cent or more over your normal training, so you will have to make some concessions in your life-style, if you are serious about the marathon. The principle I follow is that running should enlarge your life, not restrict it; but for a big challenge, you should make some sacrifices. The important runs are the two longest ones, and after these you should arrange things so that you can have a long soak in a hot bath, followed by a good meal and an early night. If you try to increase your training and have a busy life as well you will suffer for it.

The first part of the programme had no races prescribed; as you need more rest after a race they would affect the steady build-up. However, you should not go into the big event without at least one opportunity to rehearse your race-day routine. I suggest two races, the first four or five weeks before the main event and another two or three weeks before it.

They should be at least 10 miles and not more than 15 – a half-marathon or a 20km would be ideal. Treat them as part of your training, to be run at your marathon pace. Obviously you are going to try to run well, but you should not hammer yourself into the ground in the last few miles.

Mike Boit, of Kenya, one of the world's great runners, coached by the author (*courtesy Ed Lacey*)

1983 World Cross Country Championships, Gateshead. (*left to right*) Carlos Lopez, Bekele Debele, Antonio Prieto, Dave Clarke, Alberto Salazar, Alberto Cova, Pat Porter, Some Merge, Robert de Castella (*courtesy Nick Brawn*)

The author, in bare feet, on his way to winning a 5000 metres in Tokyo, 1963. Mohammed Gammoudi is fourth from the left

The essence of competition. The WAAA 1500 metres, 1982 (*courtesy Nick Brawn*)

John Robson of Scotland, in an interval training session (*courtesy Nick Brawn*)

Fast but relaxed. Christina Boxer in training (*courtesy Nick Brawn*)

Tactics are needed in today's big fields (*courtesy Nick Brawn*)

Everyone needs strength and speed. Peter Elliott and Rob Harrison in the 1982 UK v USSR match (*courtesy Nick Brawn*)

Dave Clarke in a repetition session (*courtesy Nick Brawn*)

Hills build up strength – and character (*courtesy Neil Shuttleworth*)

At the bell in the 1983 World Championship 1500 metres final. Said Aouita leads from Steve Cram, the eventual winner. Steve Ovett lies seventh (*courtesy Nick Brawn*)

Grete Waitz leads the chase after Regina Joyce (not in picture) at 22k in the Women's Marathon at the 1983 Helsinki World Championships (*courtesy Nick Brawn*)

Set yourself a schedule and try to run at level pace, as far as hills and other conditions will allow. You may well find that if you are aiming at 7-minute miles (3-hour marathon speed) it seems very easy under race conditions, but you should resist the temptation to speed up. If, after 10 miles, it still seems easy, *then* you can increase your speed. In spite of everything that is said, many, many marathons are ruined by people running too fast in the first half of the race.

The schedules set out below are the *maximum* amount of work that should be done. If in doubt, ease off a little and take it easy between the long runs. Try to cover the miles, but gently. The art of training lies in increasing the training load gradually, without losing your equilibrium and plunging into deep exhaustion.

By week 10, you are at the beginning of the run-down period to the race. The aim now is to produce good performances on two days with all other sessions subservient to those. If you are feeling tired from long runs, take the other sessions very gently, but if you are feeling good put in some bursts of strides and run strongly on the hills.

Many coaches might say that doing 20 miles with only two weeks to go was not allowing enough time to rest. If this was a *hard* 20, I would agree. A better trained runner would be ready to do 20 five weeks before the big day, and again three weeks before, with a good quality run over about 15 miles/25km with two weeks to go. In this case you are trying to go from basic level to marathon fitness in twelve weeks, so it takes ten weeks before you can safely tackle a 20.

Schedule 10. Marathon Preparation Plan:
Weeks 6 to 10

WEEK 6

Sunday:	5 miles easy
Monday:	7 miles easy – or with a few fast bursts

Tuesday: 12 miles; pace run – 10 miles,
2 miles warm-up/down
Wednesday: 6 miles easy
Thursday: 8 to 10 miles easy start, build up to fast
Friday: Rest
Saturday: 18 miles easy
Total mileage: 55 to 57

WEEK 7
Sunday: 6 miles easy
Monday: 8 miles steady, bursts on hills
Tuesday: 12 miles; pace run – 10 miles,
as above
Wednesday: 6 miles easy
Thursday: 2 × 3 miles easy; 1½ miles timed circuit
Friday: Rest
Saturday: 13 to 15 miles half-marathon
race or 15 miles steady
Total mileage: 52½ to 54½

WEEK 8
Sunday: 5* miles easy
Monday: 7* miles easy – or with fast bursts
Tuesday: 13 miles; pace run – 11 miles, as above
Wednesday: 5* miles easy
Thursday: 8 to 10* miles easy start, build up to fast
Friday: Rest
Saturday: 18 miles easy
*add 3 miles to any one day's run
Total mileage: 59 to 61

WEEK 9
Sunday: 6 miles easy
Monday: 8* miles steady, bursts on hills
Tuesday: 15 miles; pace run – 13 miles,
as above
Wednesday: 6* miles easy

Thursday: 2 × 3 miles easy; 2 × 1½ miles timed circuit
Friday: Rest
Saturday: 13 to 15 miles half-marathon race or 15 miles steady
*add 2 miles to any one day's run
Total mileage: 59 to 61

WEEK 10
Sunday: 4 miles easy
Monday: 6 miles easy
Tuesday: 6 to 8 miles fast and slow
Wednesday: 11 to 13 miles; pace run, as above
Thursday: 5 to 6 miles easy
Friday: Rest
Saturday: 20 miles comfortable
Total mileage: 51 to 56

Schedule 11. Marathon Preparation Plan: Weeks 11 and 12

WEEK 11
Sunday: 3 to 5 miles easy
Monday: 4 to 6 miles easy, some strides
Tuesday: 5 to 6 miles fast and slow, no pressure
Wednesday: 12 miles; pace run – 10 miles, 2 miles warm-up/down
Thursday: 5 to 6 miles easy
Friday: Rest
Saturday: 14 miles; 1 mile warm-up, 13 miles at marathon speed
Total mileage: 43 to 49

WEEK 12
Sunday: 3 to 5 miles easy
Monday: 3 miles easy, 2 × 1½ miles at marathon pace

Tuesday: 6 miles steady
Wednesday: 8 miles; pace run – 6 miles,
2 miles warm-up/down
Thursday: 5 miles easy, some strides
Friday: Rest or 3 miles easy
Saturday: 2 mile walk/jog A.M.
3 mile jog P.M.
Total mileage: 33 to 38

The first principle of the medical profession is 'do no harm', and this should be your motto during the last two weeks of your training for the marathon. A lot of people have the idea that if you miss a day's training you start to go downhill immediately. This would only be true if you lay in bed all day, but with light activity, walking about, going up and down stairs, your condition will not deteriorate. If you have been training hard in the previous week, you will be in better condition after two or three days' rest, and a further three days' easy running will maintain you in the same state. So, if you are prevented from serious training for a complete Monday-to-Friday period, don't panic.

The previous five weeks have probably been the hardest training of your life. At the end of this time, in spite of my good advice, you may be a little run-down. Looking over my own and others' training diaries, I have often noticed how a minor infection, such as a sore throat, or a slight muscular strain, comes after three or four weeks of progressively harder training. You must pay attention to these warnings. You are treading a delicate balance between super-fitness and over-exhaustion, so listen to your body talking.

Assuming that you managed to run 20 miles non-stop by the end of the second phase, and also assuming that you now have several half-marathons under your belt, you can be confident about finishing your big race and you will have a good idea about what sort of average mile speed you can expect to maintain. In the two-week count-down you should not run anything more than 15 seconds a mile faster than this. Successful marathon running depends on finding the right rhythm and running as economically as possible.

The most difficult question to decide is when you should make your last hard effort before the race. The international marathon runners make their last big effort with seven to nine days to go, but I see from my training diary that when I ran my best distance race (1 hour 41 minutes for the Finchley 20) I had been doing hard interval training only three days before. The most practical time for most of us is over the weekend preceding the big day. The distance should be 10 to 15 miles, done at the speed of your best possible marathon.

If you are going to go on the marathon bleed-out diet (see page 207) you will be cutting down on your carbohydrate intake, so you will not be able to do much except easy runs on those days, but if you are eating normally, I would suggest a pace run on the Wednesday before Sunday's race.

The final thing to take into account is the travelling and change of routine in the last few days. If your race starts at 9.30 A.M. and your last meal is breakfast at 6.30, you should try to rehearse this routine daily during the last week. If you have to spend most of the day before the race travelling, try to walk, stretch and jog lightly at intervals during the journey.

Final thoughts. The long run at the end of week 10 and the three pace runs should be done in the shoes and clothing you will wear on race day. This will give you time to sort out any problems. If you are expecting to drink regularly, which I recommend, you should practise this, too, because you may find that it upsets your stomach to gulp down drinks while on the run.

Two things which have not been mentioned are stretching and twice-a-day training. The former I have assumed is done daily by all serious runners. It should precede even your slow runs, while before your fast runs you should have 10 minutes of jogging so as to be thoroughly warm before you start to run fast.

For the 50 to 60 miles per week runner, training twice a day is a waste of time. The process of changing into running kit and then changing back adds 15 to 20 minutes to each session and the end result is that neither session is long enough to be of real benefit. One session is usually in the early morning, when your body is not functioning at its best. You will probably need to do at least 3 miles before you are properly warmed-up, so the training value of the early morning jog is almost nil.

When it comes to the second session you tend to cut down slightly on the full-scale training because you have reached your daily mileage quota. What really matters is the amount of good training you put in and a lot of this early morning stuff is just 'rubbish' running. It *is* worth doing for the top-class runner, because he is pushing himself hard every day and the extra easy session helps him to recover from the effects of the hard running. My final piece of advice is the one which cannot be repeated too often: however good you may feel, run the first 5 miles of the marathon itself at a level, comfortable pace.

Going further and faster

The second-year plan you have been following, if gone through properly without any hold-ups, will give you a rough idea of your marathoning ability, though it will still be a long way from your true potential, maybe 20 or 30 minutes away. Say you run a time of 3 hours 10 minutes on this schedule; how much room is there for further improvement? Look at yourself objectively. Are you overweight (compared to other marathon runners, not 'average' people)? I remember an athlete from Bournemouth, Roger Matthews, who had been running for several years as a reasonable club distance runner, training quite hard all the year round. In 1969, inspired by Dave Bedford's performances, he decided to train *really* hard. He went up to running 120 miles a week, lost about 15 pounds, and emerged as a top-class international, finishing fourth in the Commonwealth Games 10,000m in 1970. That reduction of ten per cent in his bodyweight meant, of course, that his maximum oxygen intake, in millimetres per kilogram per minute, went *up* by ten per cent. At a lower level, we achieved the same effect with a female orienteer, who was keen and skilful, but who could not run fast enough. A careful combination of weight loss and harder training made a considerable difference.

We have to be careful here, because there is some evidence that dieting while training hard can be dangerous. It would be best to tackle it in two stages – first, to control the diet, while keeping to a normal or slightly easier training regime; and then to allow harder training. What to eat when your training load increases is dealt with in Chapter 12.

If you reckon that you cannot afford to lose more weight, what then? Can you afford to spend a little more time on training? If you followed the twelve-week pattern again, but made it a sixteen-week build-up, you could repeat weeks 9 and 10 twice. This means that you would have two more 20-milers and six more runs in the 13 to 15 mile range under your belt before race day. Naturally, going at this schedule for the second time, you would feel more confident and run your pace runs a little faster.

Each marathon you run equips you better for the next one, because you learn more about your behaviour under stress. If you raced, say, five marathons in your second year (see the 'Strategy' section) and used the sixteen-week build-up for the marathon season in your third year, you could expect to keep on chipping the times down before you reach a 'plateau' level. Here the training you are doing is not enough to enable you to improve. For anyone but the very gifted, this kind of schedule will not enable you to break 2 hours 20 minutes for a man or 3 hours for a woman.

If you really want to improve, you have got to work at two factors – your average running speed and your endurance ability. It will no longer be enough just to keep fit during most of the year and build up for one or two marathon seasons. What you need is progressive training, or what some coaches call 'Periodization'. This simply means that you work on particular aspects of your running at certain times of the year, and you keep on moving onwards and upwards from one phase to another.

You are likely to be moving into serious marathon running from one of two positions. You may be a 'new wave' runner who has gone straight into road running and found that in a couple of seasons you are not far off the leading bunch; you are under 2 hours 40 (men) or under 3 hours (women). Alternatively you are a runner who has been in the world of cross-country and track for several years, perhaps since schooldays, and you have decided that as you can't make it elsewhere, you are going to try the Big M.

If you are a club distance runner you will probably have some cross-country and road relay commitments. I suggest that you stick to the Winter Training schedule in the cross-country season (see Chapter 8) with a couple of alterations. Put in a long run on Wednesdays, at least 11 miles and up to 15, and increase your total mileage by putting in four or five extra sessions of steady running a week totalling 20 miles.

If you are coming in from the world of slow steady road running, you will have to make a few adjustments, because you must get used to running fast. You are aiming to compete in *races* rather than time-trials, which means that you must have some speed. If you are hoping to run a decent marathon, down to 2 hours 20 minutes or below (2 hours 40 for women), you have got to be racing at below 5 minute 30 seconds miles. You must be able to race short distances at well under 5-minute mile speed. For women, add nearly a minute per mile to all these remarks, since the good female marathoner is about 20 minutes slower than her male counterpart over the full distance.

Assuming that you have reached the point in your basic conditioning where you are capable of running 50 to 60 miles a week, on the lines of weeks 7 and 8 in the previous twelve-week plan, you should now start to switch over to something closer to the Winter Training programme in Chapter 8. I imagine this taking place through October to December in Britain and North America, April to June in the southern hemisphere. Introduce a session of repetition running to start with, and repeat this every two weeks. Start running your 'easy' or 'steady' sessions as fast and slow sessions, putting in short bursts to start with, and gradually increasing the length of the bursts. These runs then become Fartlek sessions. Two weeks later, you can start on either hill sprints or interval training, using one of these sessions every two weeks.

In keeping with the trend towards speed, you will not be entering any races longer than 10 miles in this period. When you start on this more intensive kind of training, I suggest you give racing a miss for a month, so that your muscles have time to get used to the faster stuff, and then you can try your new self out in 5 mile or 10km races. Your two-week pattern of training will then look like this:

Schedule 12. Marathon Speed Training: Two-Week Programme

WEEK 1

Sunday: 11 to 16 miles steady

Monday: Road repetition runs, 6 × 1 mile approx., timed with 5 minutes rest between each

Tuesday: Fartlek, preferably not on road, 8 miles

Wednesday: 10-mile run with bursts up hills, or 12 to 20 × 200m hill sprints, with warm-up/down

Thursday: 5 miles easy A.M.; 5 miles fast P.M.
Friday: 4 to 5 miles easy, morning or lunch-time
Saturday: Club race or 6 miles Fartlek

WEEK 2

Sunday: 11 to 16 miles steady
Monday: Interval training, preferably not on road. 6 to 8 × 800m approx. (at least 2 minutes fast) with 2 minutes recovery jog; then 6 to 8 × 400m (or 1 minute fast), with 1 minute jog
Tuesday: 5 miles run in boots
Wednesday: 8 to 10 miles Fartlek, with bursts as you feel
Thursday: 5 miles easy A.M.; warm-up, 3 miles fast, warm-down, P.M.
Friday: Rest or 4 to 5 miles easy
Saturday: Race 5 to 10 miles

The total mileage here is only going to be 50 to 60 miles a week, but it is going to put far more stress on your system than the steady runs. You will be able to measure your improvement in the times you record your repetition runs, and in the number of fast hill runs you can manage, as well as in your race times for short distances.

Phase two: quality and quantity. Here we are getting into the real stuff, as done by the Alberto Salazars, the de Castellas and the Joan Benoits. It is not enough to run a lot of miles, they have got to be *good* miles.

If you have worked through the speed training satisfactorily, you will now be ready for the mileage build-up. This could start before Christmas in Britain and continue through to the end of March, ready for the racing peak in April/May.

It might be argued that it would be better to build up the miles in the autumn and then, having reached peak mileage, to introduce the quality training. This might be valid for the more experienced runner, but if you are trying to break into top-class marathon running without a background of track experience you really need to have a serious racing period over the shorter road distances. There is no reason, however, why you should not employ the speed training session during June to August, switch over to mileage in the autumn and then combine quantity and quality in the January to March period. One important factor is the climate, which forces you to get most of your fast work done before it turns really nasty. If you have to wear a lot of protective clothing, it may inhibit you from doing quality work but it doesn't stop you grinding out the miles.

How much mileage? As much as you can take without getting injured. If you move on from the speed training by increasing the length of the Sunday, Tuesday and Thursday runs, you will get up to 75 a week. If you put in an extra 5-mile session on Mondays, Tuesdays and Wednesdays you will add another 15, making a possible 90 miles a week. This would be enough for the first year of serious marathon running.

When you decide to increase your mileage, it is crazy to go from 60 to 90 miles a week in one jump. An increase of 10 miles is enough, and you would be advised to cut down slightly on the intensity of the hard sessions. If you can then go through the two-week cycle and feel strong, you can add another 10 miles of steady running. Once you are up to 90 miles a week, say by February, I suggest that you keep it at that level for most of the next two months and don't try any increase until you move on to the next phase. Remember, every person is a one-man experiment. You have got to give yourself a chance to see what 90 miles a week does for you before going over the 100 mark.

It is my firm belief that hard training is better for you than easy training, hence the repetition and interval work. However, once you get up to 90 miles a week you are running nearly 15 miles every day, and 20 miles once a week. There are going to be times when your glycogen reserves are too low for you to be able to run fast *and* long, and as you move nearer to marathon day the long runs become more important. The speed work occupies a smaller part of the week. You will not really have lost in quality, because by now you will be running your 10s and 15s at a faster pace. The benefits you were previously getting only from the repetition miles or the short fast runs are now being gained in most of your 'steady' runs. If you are aiming at a sub-2 hours 30 minutes marathon you will also be aiming at a sub-1 hour 10 minutes half-marathon.

By this stage you will not be running in short club races on Saturdays; instead, you will either be racing half-marathons at the weekend, or putting in a fast run in the same range, 11 to 15 miles. Your weekly pattern of running will now look like this:

Schedule 13: 90-Miles-a-Week Programme

Sunday: 15 to 20 miles slow and easy
Monday: 4 to 5 miles easy, A.M.; interval or repetition work, 8 miles total, P.M.
Tuesday: 4 to 5 miles easy, A. M.; 13 miles fast, P.M.
Wednesday: 4 to 5 miles easy, A.M.; 8 to 10 miles Fartlek, with bursts on the hills, P.M.
Thursday: 4 to 5 miles easy, A.M.; 10 miles quite fast, continuous, P.M.
Friday: 4 to 5 miles easy
Saturday: Race or trial, 10 to 13 miles
Total mileage: 85 to 90

The following is an example of training done by Joyce Smith in 1980, before setting a British marathon record of 2 hours 33 minutes, at the age of forty-two.

Schedule 14: Joyce Smith's 1980 Marathon Training

Monday: 8 to 10 miles
Tuesday: 4 × 800m, about 2 minutes 25 each

Wednesday: 18-mile run, 1 hour 53 minutes
Thursday: 9 miles, 58 minutes, A.M.; 5 miles, P.M.
Friday: 8 miles
Saturday: 25½ miles, 2 hours 44 minutes
Total mileage: 80

One of the basic rules of a training programme is that it should be building you up, not breaking you down, and it won't do this unless you get enough rest. Most runners alternate big mileage weeks with easier weeks, or at least they ease off a lot every fourth week. This, of course, usually coincides with the need to rest up before a race. A typical four-week period in this phase might therefore go: 92 miles, 80, 95, 60.

The racing season. When you reach this phase the most important thing is how you feel at the time. You cannot be dogmatic about how many miles you should run, because sometimes you will need a lot of rest after a race and at other times you will feel that you want to go out and get in a steady 20 to boost your confidence.

In the physiological sense, the training you do in the last two weeks before won't have very much effect on deep-down things like capillarization of the muscle or changes in enzyme content, but we know that there are changes in blood sugar, blood lactate and muscle glycogen, which correspond with subjective feelings about how good you are feeling. If you push yourself hard, say in a hard 15-mile run, you are going to be a bit low the next day, and if you have an easy day you will feel good the following day. The two-week run-down or 'tapering' period has to have enough running in it to make you feel confident and enough rest in it for you to be at a physical peak on the day.

In this period, training should be once a day only, preferably at the same time of day as the race. Our bodies have their cycles of higher and lower activity, but they do respond to training, and even if you are not at your best at ten in the morning you can train yourself to perform well at that time. When you do make an effort it should be a hard effort, and in between the hard efforts you should take it easy, to allow the rebuilding of fuel and the excretion of waste to occur. In the penultimate week you follow a pattern of alternate hard and easy days, increasing the amount of rest in the last week. The last really long run should be ten to fifteen days before the big day. This should be at least 20 miles and may even be the full distance, if you have enough mileage background to be able to take it – a regular 80 to 90 miles a week. This gives us a pattern like this:

Schedule 15: Marathon Preparation: Two Weeks Before the Race

WEEK 1

Sunday: Long steady run, 22 to 26 miles, trying to stay comfortable
Monday: Rest or gentle jog
Tuesday: 8 miles Fartlek, with surges on the hills
Wednesday: Rest or gentle jog
Thursday: 4 × 1½ miles at fast marathon speed
Friday: Easy jog, 3 to 4 miles
Saturday: Rest. Do something different (but not dangerous)

WEEK 2

Sunday: Fast 13 to 15 miles
Monday: Rest or easy 3-mile jog
Tuesday: Steady 6 to 8 miles
Wednesday: Warm-up, 1 mile, then 10 miles at marathon speed
Thursday: 5 miles, starting easy, with a few stride-outs
Friday: Rest or 3 to 4 miles easy
Saturday: Easy 3 to 4 miles after travelling
Sunday: The Marathon

Onwards and upwards. Arthur Lydiard deservedly gets the credit for making the '100-miles-a-week' regime the accepted one for long distance runners. It is hard to fit more than this into a working week, and harder still to combine quality training with high mileage. However, if we look at marathon running without any preconceptions at all, we can see that 100 miles a week is some way short of the ideal training for the marathon. In all other events, runners and swimmers cover far more distance in their daily training than they do in a race. It can be done. Dave Bedford went up to 200 miles a week; it destroyed him, but that was because he went up too quickly, and he did become world record holder for 10,000m. The leading marathon men in the world are now running 140 miles a week, and the ultra-marathon men are doing more than that. In countries where the foot is the only method of travel, 40 miles in a day is not an excessive distance, but it is done slowly, taking eight to ten hours. When I ran from Los Angeles to New York, I got into a regular routine of 48 to 50 miles a day, which involved about seven hours of running. When I got used to it, I felt I could keep it up for months, but it was *very* boring! Way back in 1922, that pioneer of long distance, Arthur Newton, ran 9000 miles in his first year of training. Think about that! He was then in his late thirties, toughened by years of farming life in Africa, but it is still an amazing figure.

The only reason that modern runners are not doing 200 miles a week or more is that they are not brought up to using their legs a lot from an early age, and they are conditioned by the educational and economic system into allowing only one or two hours a day for recreational activities such as running. If I had a free hand to train marathon runners regardless of anything else, I would get them on to running 30 miles a day at the age of eighteen, with 40-mile runs on the long days. After two or three years of this, a 26-mile race would seem a mere dash, as it does to the Tarahumara Indians. For the latter, the big race is the 160 mile cross-country! The thing you need is time, because you start by getting used to walking 30 miles a day before you run it, and time is what primitive man had plenty of, but modern man very little.

To come down to practical terms, there is no reason why the really ambitious runner, doing a part-time job, or being unemployed for part of the year, should not be putting in 150 miles a week. The most significant aspect of de Castella's training is the long run, 30 to 35 miles, which he puts in three weeks or more before his big race. On ordinary days, the international is running twice a day, with at least one of those sessions being hard. Looking at the schedules of John Graham, Hugh Jones and Alberto Salazar, all of them sub-2 hours 10 performers, one finds that they all do interval and repetition training, they all run fast 10-milers at a pace close to their best marathon pace, and they all do two runs a week in the 2 hours to 2 hours 30 range.

It is up to the ambitious runner to keep building up, from season to season, improving quantity and quality step-by-step, looking for the pattern which suits him best. He has got to accept that it will take five years, and maybe ten, to reach his full potential.

Marathon strategy

In your first year you will probably try the event a couple of times, and in the second year, with more regular mileage behind you, you might try a couple of events in the spring and a couple in the autumn. When you decide to take it seriously, you need to decide which races you are going for and plan a racing programme accordingly. You need to include the following training phases:

1 Background mileage
2 Speed training

3 Quality and quantity
4 Race preparation
5 Recovery from racing season.

When you are into your routine, the recovery period from one racing season will merge into the background mileage – steady unpressured running – of the following one. With roughly two months each on phases 2 and 3, it should be possible to have two racing seasons a year, each including two or three marathons. The first marathon could be included as part of the training in phase 3, just to convince yourself that you can handle the distance comfortably, without injury. The other two races should be considered as all-out, win-or-bust efforts, in which you are committed to getting the best possible result from your training and preparation, and after one of those you will need at least six weeks before you can produce another. A very good and very experienced man, like Bill Rodgers, *can* go on running races every two or three weeks for a few months, but some of those races are bound to be mediocre. Of course, the fitter you are the more races you can handle.

At the lower end of the spectrum, you can run plenty of marathons if you are just *running* them, not racing them. When I was running across America, I ran a marathon every morning for the last forty days, but they were slow 3 hours 30 min. runs. What is slow for one person is flat out for another, so you cannot lay down rules about 'how often'. One man has run a marathon every week for fifty-two weeks, and in 1983 a doctor, who should have known better, ran the London Marathon and the Boston Marathon on consecutive days. We're all crazy, but some are crazier than others!

Tactics. Van der Merwe, the man they tell all the jokes about, was painting his fence. As the neighbour came by, he said, 'Van der Merwe, you're working very fast; what's the hurry?' 'I'm running out of paint, man, so I'm trying to get the job finished before the can's empty!' It sounds crazy, I know, but how many of us run a marathon on that principle? The reasoning goes: 'I'm bound to slow down later, so if I go faster at the beginning I'll have a bit in hand.'

What is it that slows you down in a marathon? If you look back to Chapter 5, you will see that there are two main factors – running out of fuel and overheating.

Any race longer than 15 miles is a fuel economy run. You have got to think, the whole way, about being as gentle on the pedal as possible. When talking about fuel supplies, I use the analogy of a fuel tank which is being supplied by a trickle of fuel from the mobilization of fat. There is some evidence that this fat mobilization does not really get going at its maximum level at the start, so this is another reason for starting at a level pace.

In most races, whoever you are, there are going to be people in front of you and people behind you. To get the best out of yourself you have to know what you are aiming to do.

Estimating your time. This will probably only be necessary for the first-time runner, because from then on you have a pretty good idea of your state of fitness as compared with other races. Obviously it is related to your basic running speed; someone who can run a 6-minute mile comfortably is bound to run a marathon faster than someone who can only manage a 7-minute mile, if both have done the same amount of endurance training. You can therefore use your times from slower races to predict your marathon. A number of rules of thumb were given in *Running* magazine (June 1982) and I have added some of my own, to make up Table 2.

The shorter the distance you are using, the greater your chance of a false estimate. A young athlete, or one who is naturally quite fast, might record a good time for 5 miles, but not have the necessary background to produce the

Table 2. Estimating Your Time

Known distance	Multiplying factor
5 miles	6
6 miles	5
10 miles	3
13.1 miles (half-marathon)	2, plus 10 minutes
10km	4.66
20km	2.1, plus 10 minutes
20 miles	1.33

corresponding marathon time. The conversion from short distance can only hold good if, during the four weeks leading up to the race, excluding the 'tapering period', you have averaged 60 miles a week, and have had at least two runs of 20 miles. It is obvious that multiplying your best 5-mile time by six is going to give you a better predicted marathon time than three times your 10-mile performance, but these are only approximations for the inexperienced. If you use all the available information, and bear in mind that not all courses are alike, nor are they accurately measured, you will have an idea of what you hope to run in your first full marathon.

Planning your pace. Based on the above paragraphs, you will have an estimated time. You will also have in your mind a 'dream time', which is the best you could possibly hope for, and a 'rock bottom', which is a time which you would be disappointed not to beat. The speed you should go off at should be as close as possible to the average speed for your estimate, because this will not rule out your chances of the dream time. If you go off at dream time pace, and have a bad day, there is a good chance of your failing to beat the rock bottom time, or of not finishing at all.

For example, say you have run a 5-mile race in a shade under 29 minutes, and 10 miles in an hour. Your estimated time is somewhere between 2 hours 53 minutes and 3 hours.

Your dream time is 2 hours 45 minutes and your rock bottom is 3 hours 10 minutes. The right speed to start at is around 6 minutes 40 per mile, which will get you to 5 miles in just over 33 minutes. If you find yourself running really well, you can speed up gradually, reaching 10 miles in one hour 5 and 20 miles in 2 hours 8 or 9, which just puts you within reach of your dream time. On the other hand, if you are not in your best form, or the conditions are against you, you may be slowed down to 7-minute miles. In this case, a starting pace of 6 minutes 40 per mile is not too foolhardy.

For beginners, the adage to remember is: '20 miles is only halfway.' You must just nurse yourself through the first 10, and then think of getting to the half-marathon point on schedule, then to 15 miles and then to 20. Remember that for the first couple of races, finishing is more important than time, and have patience. If you have, in fact, underestimated your ability, it is surprising and gratifying to find how much ground one can pick up over the last 6 miles, and I do not recommend attempting any kind of 'charge' until the 20-mile mark.

For the more able runner the problem is different. You are running, let us say, in the 2 hours 30 to 2 hours 35 range. This puts you in with a chance of a trophy or an age-group award in everything except the really big races. You know your local rivals, but there will be others around you in the race whom you don't know. You go off at your scheduled speed, and after the first couple of miles you see that a group in front of you, including some of your known rivals, are starting to move away. Do you go with them, sacrificing your level pace schedule for the advantage of having someone to hang on to? My advice is to stick to your own pace. Look at the reports of races when the Boston Marathon and the Olympics were being won in those sorts of times. Time after time you read about runners 'blowing up' in the later stages. Economy of effort is what matters.

The problem of running in the early part of the race is that the true limiting factors have not started to apply. You are not hot or dehydrated, you have plenty of fuel. Your average marathon miling speed is much slower than your best mile, so you feel comfortable and, at the same time, the thrill of the race is urging you to go faster, not to let those people go past you. You will need all your experience and self-control to stick to your schedule in the early stages. A little devil of temptation is whispering in your ear: 'You can run faster than this. Why don't you just blow these people away? You're in shape to run 2 hours 20!' Stay cool. If you are running at about 5 minutes 40 seconds a mile, which is just under the 2 hours 30 speed, and you are *really* capable of 2 hours 20, then you are bound to finish well under 2 hours 30 and run a personal best; and you can go for a faster time in your next race. You have a whole lifetime ahead of you, so just be satisfied to be on schedule. When it comes to the last 6, you will need all your fighting spirit.

The pattern of present-day marathon running is becoming much more like that of long distance track races. In the old days, everyone blasted off and those who were the fittest slowed down the least. In the clash between Peters and Zátopek mentioned in Chapter 2, Peters went off at a terrific speed, running at 5-minute mile speed for the first few miles. At 10km, in spite of slowing a lot, he clocked 31 minutes 55, 20 seconds ahead of Zátopek. At 20km, Zátopek's time was 64 minutes 27, so his second 10km was exactly the same speed as his first, but Peters was by then 10 seconds behind. Zátopek reached halfway in just over 68 minutes, and finished in 2 hours 23, demolishing the previous Olympic record, but Peters collapsed and came back in an ambulance. He was brave but stupid. You cannot expect to drop the Olympic 5000m champion in the early stages of the race. The time to drop him is in the last 6 miles.

The type of race we see now, as, for example, in the 1983 Rotterdam Marathon, is a fast-level pace in the early stages, followed by tactical bursts, using the hills, in the second half. As in a 10,000m race, one is liable to finish up with a leading group of two or three and the man with the sprint finish sitting in while the others try to break away. In a race of this distance, however, the possession of a sprint finish is of little value compared to conditioning. If you are looking for the likely winner, it is going to be the man who has the best record over the last 7km of the race. A course like Boston is an exception, because the long climb and the fast downhill, all between miles 19 and 22, usually decide the race, but even here you sometimes get sprint finishes, as in 1982, when Salazar beat Beardsley. If you compare times over the last few miles for flattish courses such as London, Fukuoka and New York, you can see who are the best men. Looking at recent years, the fastest race from 35km to the finish was the 1983 Rotterdam Marathon, where de Castella clocked 21 minutes 2, closely followed by Lopes. This works out at an average of 4 minutes 40 seconds per mile for the last 4½ miles. The next fastest man is Cierpinski in Moscow, 1980.*

In the next four years, I think that we shall see the 2 hours 6 marathon. It will be run with every 5km stretch between 15 minutes and 15 minutes 20 until the 35km mark, when they will speed up to a sub-15 minutes pace, reaching 40km in just over 2 hours and then kicking in the last 2km in well under 6 minutes. The man who is going to do that is going to have the complete armoury of track speed, great endurance, heat tolerance, pace judgement and, of course, tremendous strength of mind. He could be American, British, Australian, Finnish, African, South American, Mexican or Japanese. A great runner is a source of pride not for one nation, but for the whole world.

*It is significant that these two, finishing first and third in the 1983 World Championships, have the best record in championship events.

8

The Cross-Country Runner

Cross-country running is the most natural and uninhibited form of our sport. As practised in Britain at school and club level, it involves all types of terrain – sometimes easy running on playing fields or roads, sometimes diabolically difficult running over frozen rutted plough or through knee-deep swamp. When you come to championship level, the size of the field creates the need for smooth open ground for the first part of the race at least, so these races are often held in large parks or race-courses, which make them a bit easier for the track runner. In general, however, the existence of mud, hills and fences in the course makes this branch of the sport physically tougher than road or track.

Mentally, cross-country is much easier. A lot of the time it is a real pleasure to run through the English countryside, on a course marked by old trees, woodland paths and the natural rise and fall of the land. Running in natural conditions always makes me feel in tune with the surroundings, whereas road and track are hostile environments, to be fought against.

Cross-country runners are a different sub-set of the running population. Little glamour surrounds their races. Except for big championship races there are no spectators, just a few girlfriends or relatives, loyal beyond the call of duty, trying to keep their circulations going while the runners disappear into the distance, and trying to summon up enthusiasm when they return, covered in mud, half an hour later. The strange thing, to the uninitiated spectator, who is probably feeling cold in spite of wellington boots and sheepskin coat, is that the runners, in shorts and T-shirts, are not only glowing with heat when they finish, but they actually enjoy it, at least in retrospect. Some may call it masochism, or the beating-your-head-against-a-brick-wall complex, but there is great satisfaction in cross-country racing and training. To run hard, in spite of wind and rain, to slog through mud, to push yourself up the last hill and then keep hammering it all the way to the finish, is a great way of asserting your individuality. Even if there are only a couple of dozen people there, you are witnesses to each other's efforts. You know you have done it and they know that you have done it, and whatever else you may have done that day, it has not been wasted. The enjoyment of a hot bath after the run, followed by tea beside the fire, combines the pleasures of many senses. It is, I feel, a very British experience which we share with the racing fraternity, from where the sport derived, in the middle of the nineteenth century.

In the very early days of Thames Hare and Hounds, the first cross-country club, races took the form of paper-chases, but the fixed course soon become the rule. The English championships were originally over 10 miles, which meant at least an hour's running, and 'The National', the English Cross-Country Union club and individual championships are still over 9 miles, as are the area championships. The majority of club races, however, are in the 5- to 7-mile range, with county championships nominally over 7½ miles.

The pattern of the year in Britain is that club cross-country matches and leagues start about mid-October and run to early December. There is then a slight lull for Christmas, and the county championships for men are held on the first Saturday in January. Women's county championships are usually held in December, and both men's and women's organizations have their area championships in February, followed by national championships in March and world championships in mid-March. League and club matches go on through all weathers except very severe snow and ice, finishing in early March. The six months of October to March thus provide a competitive season which alternates precisely with the outdoor track season and, before the growth of the importance of road running, most British runners went from track to cross-country and back again. In Europe the situation was much the same, particularly in the strong cross-country areas of Belgium and northern France, but in North America the cross-country season still means the period from mid-September to Thanksgiving, after which the indoor track season claims the attention of those not involved in road racing.

It is generally agreed that Britain's strength in distance running stems from the cross-country tradition. The relatively mild winters enable us to train out of doors all the year round, and the cross-country races give us the incentive to train on soft ground, which is much easier on the legs than roads are. At the top level, the pressures of competition have become so great that the leading track runners and marathon runners cannot combine their training with a full winter racing programme. At club level, however, there is no reason at all why one should not combine track and cross-country with success, or road and cross-country. The idea of the sport is to get fit and enjoy our fitness by racing, and cross-country fills the bill very well. Because of the lack of prizes and publicity, the people who do it are modest and genuine – though they can be pretty aggressive in the heat of the race!

If you are coming into club cross-country for the first time, you will need a few weeks of steady running just to get your muscular system accustomed to different stresses. If you have a tendency towards weakness in the knees or ankles, I recommend regular long walks before the season starts. As the English season doesn't get going until well into October, there is plenty of chance to get out walking or jogging over the fields as soon as the harvest is over, and before the autumn ploughing is done. If you are tackling American cross-country in September, I suggest toughening up your knees and ankles by running on the beach in August.

Basic cross-country training

To perform respectably, even at the lower club level, you have got to be running 30 to 40 miles a week. You will have to include a bit of everything – stamina work, speed work, and different types of going, but in particular you will have to do hill training, because it is on the hills that races are won and lost. A typical week's training will look something like this:

Schedule 16: Basic Cross-Country Training

Sunday: Long slow run, 6 to 12 miles
Monday: Jog out to hills, 12 × 100m up 1 in 10 slope, run back
Tuesday: Club night. 6 to 7 mile run with group, starting slow finishing fast
Wednesday: Fartlek run round 6-mile course
Thursday: Warm-up for 1 mile, then 3 to 4 mile fast road run
Friday: Rest, or circuit training in gym
Saturday: Club cross-country race 5 to 7 miles

The above schedule, as you can see, has only one day of slow running, which is the day after Saturday's race. On all the other days, something different but useful is being done. The beginner may need some time to work up to this, and should start by alternating hard days with steady jogging over the 4 to 6 mile distance.

This type of training, with regular races, will keep you progressing through your first year of cross-country. If you have ambitions to run in, say, the northern championships, you will need to increase your mileage in order to perform properly over a 9-mile course. You will also want to find different places to run and more demanding types of training, as you continue to develop. In Chapter 4 I described the main types of training which are used, and the all-round cross-country runner will need to use all of these. If he or she is planning to use this Winter Programme as a build-up to the racing season in the summer, plenty of variety is equally necessary, to strengthen up all the systems that are used.

Two kinds of training are particularly useful to the ambitious cross-country runner – boots running and resistance running. The greatest British cross-country runner of recent times was undoubtedly Dave Bedford. Those of us who were there will never forget his feat of winning the Southern Counties senior title – a 9-mile race against 500 competitors – and then turning out 20 minutes later to win the under-twenty-one race over 6 miles against another 400 fresh athletes. Dave Bedford used to train in boots regularly – though not all the time – and so did Emil Zatopek. It is hard work, but if you can get used to running 10 miles at a good pace in a heavy pair of boots, everything else is going to seem pretty easy. It has been shown that, in running, the greatest amount of effort is expended in pulling the feet through on each stride, hence the insistence on having light racing shoes. If your leg and hip muscles have to get used to pulling an extra pound on each foot, they are going to become stronger and better supplied with blood. The same effect is obtained by using ankle weights. You have to be careful not to use these all the time, because it will distort your running action.

Resistance running over a longish course (at least 1000m)

will give the cross-country runner the benefits of repetition running, the extra leg-work derived from running on soft ground and a general strengthening of the posture muscles. It is also specific event training, inculcating the running style needed to run fast and efficiently over rough ground. When you look at the great cross-country men, they seem to glide effortlessly while others are stumbling about and rocking from side to side. This is because their muscular system is absorbing the shock and automatically correcting the amount of drive on each stride – a sort of independent front suspension.

Suitable terrain for resistance would be sand, such as the tracks used for horses in winter, rough grass, or a 'jogging trail' made of wood shavings laid over a mud path. Some of my Cambridge friends used to train over sticky ploughed fields, but this is too much of a good thing. In winter you can use soft snow in the park.

Putting these things together and increasing the mileage will give you a training pattern on the following lines:

Schedule 17. Winter Training: Two-Week Programme

WEEK 1

Sunday: 10 to 14 mile run, easy pace

Monday: Road repetitions, 6 × 1 mile approx., timed, with 5 minutes rest between each

Tuesday: Fartlek round 8-mile circuit; 2 miles steady, then 1 minute fast, 1 minute slow, for 5 miles, last mile easy

Wednesday: Hill training, on grass. 8 × 200m up a 1 in 10 slope, plus 2 miles jogging and striding

Thursday: 5-mile road run at fast pace

Friday: 4-mile jog, morning or lunch-time

Saturday: Club c-c race

WEEK 2
Sunday: 15-mile road circuit, easy pace
Monday: 5-mile run in boots
Tuesday: Interval/repetition training on grass, 4 × 1200m (600m jog int.), at lunch-time; 4 miles in evening
Wednesday: 8 to 10 miles Fartlek, bursts up hills and according to how you feel
Thursday: 7-mile road run, with hard 3-mile stretch in the middle
Friday: Rest
Saturday: Race

Everyone will have his or her own pattern, and the distance of your road and cross-country circuits depends on what is available, but the principle is one of variety, repeating each session every two weeks. As the winter goes by you should be running the repetition sessions faster and increasing the number of the hill runs.

What about training twice a day? If you put in an extra morning or lunch-time session of 3 to 4 miles it will build up your general endurance, but I believe in getting the most out of the once-a-day training before putting in any more. Substituting two mediocre sessions for one good may make your mileage look impressive, but it won't make you run faster.

There is a lot of work in this schedule. Before major races you should reduce the amount of really hard work, cutting out the Thursday run and reducing either the Tuesday or the Wednesday. After a big race do not start hard training again until you feel fresh.

Cross-country racing tactics

There is really only one tactical decision to be made in a cross-country race. Do you go off with the leading bunch and try to hang on to a good position, or do you start at a level pace and try to come through? Experience shows that nine times out of ten the winner comes from the bunch which is leading at the end of the first mile. The person who has the pace judgement to run the middle of the race slightly faster than the leaders is very rare indeed. There are some who are so lacking in fast twitch fibres that they cannot run the first quarter of a mile as fast as the leaders, however hard they try, but they turn this deficiency into an advantage by continuing to run as hard as they can for the first 2 or 3 miles. The trouble with coming from behind in a big race is that you may have to pass 200 people on a fairly narrow course with a lot of bends and obstacles. The extra effort of all these passing manoeuvres may outweigh the advantage of starting at a level pace.

I always tell my runners that no medals are awarded for the leaders at 200 yards. I also tell them that most races are decided by the time a third of the race has been run. This means that in a school match the race is largely decided by the end of the first mile, and in a championship race, which is normally three laps of 2½ to 3 miles, it is mostly decided in the first lap.

The excitement of sport, however, is that for every ploy there is a counter-ploy, and this is true of cross-country. Before a recent school match I said to my lads: 'Racing is all a matter of bluff. You have got to convince the opposition that you are better than them, so I want you to put a really big effort in for the first mile, and by the time you get to Heartbreak Hill they will have given up.' However, the rival coach had said to his team: 'Marlborough are bound to go off fast on their own course, so don't panic. When they get to Heartbreak Hill they are bound to slow down, so after the hill I want each of you to try and work past his opponent.' With a small field of only two or three teams it is possible to do this, and his level-pace plan worked perfectly, because his runners were mentally prepared for what was going to happen. We were lucky to win the match, due to the fact that one of their scoring six was missing, and their seventh man was weak.

This brings me to the importance of mental approach, even in something as simple and physical as cross-country. We know that the leading runners appreciate how good they are, and have some sort of a race plan, for example: 'Belt off and stay with them', 'Use my strength on the hills', 'Use my speed on the fast stretches and economize in the heavy going', but the coach and the team captain often forget that the tail-end runners have a very vague idea of what is expected of them, apart from, 'Get out and do your best'.

It is obvious that in a six-to-score team race the sixth and seventh man have a vital role. If you are running in a league race of 150 runners, your best man will finish, say, in the first six, and the third and fourth men will be aiming for a place in the first thirty, and will therefore fight like hell to avoid slipping below thirty-seventh place at the worst. Your sixth and seventh men, however, either because they are youngsters, or because they haven't raced regularly during the season, are not quite sure whether they are going to finish sixtieth or one hundred and twentieth. Somebody in the team has got to point out to them, first, that they *are* the vital scoring members of the team, because they may think that they are just non-scoring extras. The next step is to plant the idea in their minds that they are *going* to finish in the first sixty and that if they finish lower than seventy-fifth they will be letting everybody down. Here the coach or captain needs to use a little subtlety, employing the 'whip and carrot' approach, dangling the carrot of the medals or the league title, while implying that if they let the team down they will probably never be asked to run again (unless the club needs them) and that they and their children will probably become the laughing stock of the neighbourhood.

Minor tactical points. Before the race, do your warm-up over the last part of the course, so that everyone knows where to start his run-in to the finish. If possible, go round the whole course beforehand, so that no one is suddenly destroyed by encountering an unexpected hill. At certain points, e.g., boggy ground, sudden turns, it is worth practising the best line to follow. Before the 1983 world cross-country championships, the Ethiopian team spent an entire week training over the course, practising running up and down the short, steep slopes.

If you are going to a strange course, bring every type of footwear. I once went to a so-called cross-country in Madrid which turned out to be ninety per cent road. Conversely, I have been to races which say 'unsuitable for spikes' and it has turned out that this means that there is a couple of hundred yards of road on each lap, which you can easily run in spikes, or that the person who wrote the instructions walked round the course in November, when it was bone-hard, and two months later the tracks have a quarter-inch film of greasy mud which makes it impossible to run *without* spikes. If you have a pair of lightweight studs you will be able to cope with most courses.

It is always best to bring too much clothing rather than too little. A lightweight nylon 'rain-suit' over your track suit is marvellous for keeping out the wind, not only when you are warming-up, but also when you are wet, cold and tired after the race, and need to be kept warm.

Should one wear a hat, gloves, an extra shirt when running in cold weather? If it is really cold, the extra blood needed to keep your arms warm may detract slightly from your racing performance. On the other hand, if you get too hot, blood may be diverted to the skin for cooling purposes. Often the best compromise is to wear a woolly hat and gloves for the first lap, but not an extra shirt. Wearing a hat, in particular, is a very good way of keeping warm and if you get too hot it is easy to throw it to a spectator. Incidentally, if you can't afford all these extra items of clothing, join in a big road race in the winter. You will find enough discarded hats, gloves, old socks and baggy T-shirts to keep an entire Dr Barnardo's Home warm for three months.

Having a good cross-country season is partly a matter of survival. It is often not the best runner who wins the league, nor the best ten men who make the England team, but those who survive the rigours of weekly racing in the British winter. It is worth spending some thought on common-sense things such as your travelling arrangements to and from the race, keeping warm after it, getting a warm shower, food and drink.

If you do pick up a cough or a cold, which is easy to do when your resistance is low, don't try to run twice as hard to make it go away. Substitute a short jog for your regular training session and give yourself a chance to recover. Missing four or five days' training is not a disaster, but getting a severe dose of 'flu might well be.

Fell running

This might be considered a form of cross-country, but actually it is more of a religion. Some southerners maintain that it is more of a disease, and that you will only take up fell running after being bitten by another fell runner, which is not unlikely, as they are a bunch of animals!

To be a good fell runner you have to have legs like tree trunks, for the 1000 feet climb, a heart like an elephant to supply said legs with blood, specially reinforced knees and ankles for the descent and you have to be more than usually courageous. It also helps if you live north of Wolverhampton.

If you think that you have these qualities or would like to develop them, fell racing offers a tremendous challenge. There is now a regular circuit of fell races over a wide range of distances, some of them longer than a marathon in running time, and there is a European Cup, which includes races in Britain, France, Germany, Austria, Switzerland and Italy. To get information about races, I suggest that you write to: The Membership Secretary, Fell Runners Association, 165 Penistone Road, Kirkburton, Huddersfield HD8 0PH.

Orienteering

Since the reader is seriously interested in running, it is unlikely that he will not have heard about orienteering, which is well established throughout Britain. Every running enthusiast should have a go at this branch of the sport. It demands a complex blend of qualities, and until you have tried several events you won't know whether or not you are suited to it. Curiously enough, the qualities which make the successful orienteer are not the same as those which make the successful cross-country runner, although orienteering involves running similar distances across country.

The mark of the great orienteer is his ability to sustain mental alertness under increasing physical pressure. In a really desperate racing situation, the successful orienteer keeps his cool, while the successful cross-country runner loses it. The successful runner needs to be slightly unbalanced, because there are times when he goes beyond the bounds of reason and pushes himself to the limit of exhaustion – Salazar is the supreme example in our era. The successful orienteer has to be balanced and has always to stay within the bounds of reason. He runs through trackless forest, relying on his map, his memory and his sense of direction (and occasionally on his compass). As he navigates his way to a control, he is simultaneously figuring out what that control will look like when he reaches it, and which way he will run out of the control after he has punched his card. He is considering how far he is round the course, how much difficult going lies ahead, and how far he can afford to push himself towards exhaustion. He has to cut out the distractions of other runners going through the forest in different directions, because he knows that some of them will be running different courses, and he has to be confident in his own judgement.

For his physical preparation, the serious orienteer would do well to follow the same type of programme as that of the cross-country runner, but he must add to that mental drills on map memory and bearings and 'situation drills' which combine the basic skills of pace counting and running on a bearing with the physical discipline of running fast through woods. It is impossible to achieve perfection, and that is why it is such a satisfying sport. It is also a world-wide sport, and more information about events in Britain and overseas can be obtained by writing to: British Orienteering Association Office, 41 Dale Road, Matlock, Derbyshire DE4 3LT.

9
The Middle Distance Track Runner

This chapter deals with flat races from 800m (half a mile) to 2000m (roughly 1¼ miles). Three thousand metre races and 2-mile races are usually run by people who specialize in longer distances, and the limiting factors in the 3000m flat and the 3000m steeplechase are much more similar to those of the 5000m than they are to the mile or the 1500m, so they are covered in Chapter 10.

What makes the middle distances so special is that they are halfway between the sprints and the true distance events. The great miler posseses qualities which are admired by the sprinter and the long distance runner, as well as by the general public. A schoolboy athlete or a fit young man can run round one lap of the track in under a minute, but it is a flat-out effort. He can therefore appreciate what is involved in running four laps in an average of less than 57 seconds each, which is what the present mile record involves.

The commonly accepted differential between a mile and a 1500m race is 18 seconds. A 3 minutes 42 seconds 1500m is regarded as equivalent to a mile in 4 minutes, but for the 5-minute miler, the difference can be taken as 20 seconds. Throughout this chapter I shall refer to miling speed, because that is still more meaningful to the majority than 1500m speed, and of course it divides easily by four, for lap times. The 400m lap is slightly shorter than the 440-yard lap, and takes half a second less time to run for the 5-minute miler. In the 800m/800 yards events, the metric distance takes about 0.8 less time to run. The lap times given in all schedules refer to the 400m track.

What makes training for the middle distances so interesting is that they are partly aerobic and partly anaerobic events (see Chapter 5). During part of the race the athlete will be going into oxygen debt, which will be repaid by heavy breathing after the race. This means that his anaerobic system of obtaining energy is very important in an 800m race, because about half of his energy will be derived from that source. In the 1500m, the anaerobic proportion is much smaller, only about twenty-five per cent, but it is in the last part of the race, when the runner is going deeper into oxygen debt, that the race is won or lost. At the same time, since the athlete is running at a speed well above the maximum intake level, the efficiency of his oxygen intake is very important too.

Stride length is important for the middle distance runner – there is no such thing as a top-class middle distance man with a short stride – so leg strength, ankle strength and flexibility of all the joints are important. As a result, although the distances they run are short, the amount of time that the athletes need to spend on training is as much as for a long distance runner.

You have only to look at the world leaders to realize that there is no single road to success. At the time of writing, Britain ranks top in the world even above the USA, by virtue of holding the men's Olympic, European and Commonwealth titles at 1500m, the Olympic 800m title, and all the world records from 800m to 2000m. On the other hand, the USSR holds all the women's records, and within the last twenty years these events have been dominated in turn by the Australians, the New Zealanders, the Kenyans and the Finns. However, such is the speed of information communication, that there is a considerable amount of 'poaching' going on. The British learned a lot from the Cerrutty and Lydiard schools of coaching, and Lydiard himself coached the Finns for a while. The Kenyan successes were due to a combination of natural ability and competitive flair, with British coaching in the early days. The intelligent coach and athlete learns from everyone, experiments, and finds out what works best for him or her.

Although we are learning more and more about *why* certain types of training work, the actual methods of training have not changed much in the last ten years. The improvements in the records are due to more intense competition, which has in turn led to a greater volume of training over a longer period of time. Unfortunately, it seems more and more that you have to be a full-time athlete to succeed at world level, but let us not forget that Sebastian Coe got his world records and an Olympic title while taking a degree at the same time.

The 6-minute miler

This is for the person who has just started running and is thinking about trying some short distances. Assuming that you have had a few months of regular jogging, followed by my Jogger-into-Runner schedule, you can start straight in by doing a 'jogger's mile'.

Time-trials and measured training sessions should be done on a track, because this will give you an objective result. Times done on somebody's stretch of road or grass can be misleading. In most of my schedules for road and cross-country runners I say that the exact distance of a training course does not really matter – what matters is improving your times on it. This remains true, but for track racing you need to develop a sense of pace judgement, and your training has got to be closely related to your event.

In the 'jogger's mile' you simply run four laps of the track at a speed which you think you can maintain all the way. Let us say that you come up with a time of 6 minutes 15 seconds. This gives us just a 'bench mark'. It gives us an idea of where to start, but it is a long way from being your best time. It is sometimes very hard for a runner, when he has run a race or a time-trial, and worked quite hard to record a certain time, to imagine that he can run, say, a minute faster for a mile. It seems quite impossible. This is where the coach's experience comes in. I know that there are many factors involved in running, and that most of them will yield to progressive training. I also know from my own experience that it *is* possible to change from a 6-minute miler to a 5-minute miler, and from a 5-minute miler to a 4-minute miler.

Middle distance training, like everything else, is partly mental and partly physical. As well as training your body to run faster you are also training your mind to cope with the increasing stress. If I run a lap of the track in, say, 75 seconds, it feels quite hard – that is to say, I am breathing quite heavily and feeling mild discomfort. However, I know that I can survive this, and so I can run two laps or three laps at that speed, suffering more and more discomfort. Because I have been through this discomfort before, I accept it as part of the business of getting fitter. If my pulse rate was being monitored as I ran, it would probably be reading about 150 beats per minute at the end of the first lap, over 160 at the end of the second lap, and 180 after three laps. When I was younger and fiercely ambitious, I could drive myself much harder in a training session, so that my pulse rate was over 200 at the end of each hard run.

As you get fitter, running is not going to feel any easier, because you are going to be running faster. The advantage of doing regular timed sessions on a track is that you can see how much you are improving. Large mileages are not essential if your aim is just to improve your short distance times, in fact they may be counter-productive. Steve Ovett may run 100 miles in a week's training, but he is fit enough to take it, and he has built up to that distance over many years. Roger Bannister broke the 4-minute mile on a training mileage of about 25 miles a week, so this is plenty for somebody who is operating in the 5- to 6-minute range.

The track season in Britain lasts from May to September, so with a basis of fitness from cross-country or road running in the winter, you can start in April, and get in four weeks of training before your first race. After that you can keep on training and racing throughout the summer, and if it is your first season, you should go on improving for most of that time, though eventually you will reach a sort of plateau, where your times will remain much the same. The training pattern in this first year should be along these lines:

Schedule 18. Middle Distance Training

Day 1: Steady run, 5 to 7 miles
Day 2: Interval training on track. 4 × 400m at miling speed, with 1 lap (400m) jog recovery, in under 3 minutes. 5 minutes rest, then repeat 4 × 400m
Day 3: Thorough warm-up, then 1 × 200m approx. on grass or sand, with 1 to 2 minutes rest between each. Speed should be appreciably faster than day 2
Day 4: Easy run, 3 to 5 miles
Day 5: 1 mile jog, then 3 long bursts of 3 minutes fast running, untimed, on any surface, with 4 to 5 minutes' rest after each burst. 1 mile warm-down

Every other week, substitute a time-trial instead of day 5. This time-trial can be over two laps, three laps or four laps of the track. The weather and track conditions, the time of each lap, and your personal reactions, should be recorded each time (see Chapter 3). This is important, because you might run a 5 minute 30 second mile on one occasion, in good conditions, with someone setting a nice level pace for you. Another time you might go out on your own, on a cold windy day, run a fast first lap, then slow down, and still run 5 minutes 30. This would indicate that you had improved, because in an ideal situation you would probably run 5 minutes 20, or better.

The approximate speeds at which you should be running on the interval training day are shown in the following table.

Table 3. Interval Training Summary

Best mile time	equivalent time for 1500 metres	approx. speed per lap, for intervals
6 mins 20	6.00 mins	90–94 secs
6 mins 00	5 mins 40	85–89 secs
5 mins 40	5 mins 20	80–84 secs
5 mins 20	5 mins 00	79–79 secs
5 mins 00	4 mins 40	72–75 secs

The other two quality sessions in this week's training are designed to improve your basic speed, by developing skill, stride length and co-ordination while running fast 200m stretches, and to develop mental strength and physical endurance by keeping yourself under pressure in the long 3-minute bursts.

When the racing season starts, stick to this pattern. You will probably be racing on a Saturday, so you should do two quality sessions a week, on Monday and Wednesday, or on a Tuesday and Thursday. Choose any two out of the three given.

If things go according to plan, your times for the short distances should improve rapidly in the first few weeks of racing. The ideal situation would be to race over a mile/1500m about twice a month, and to fit in a race over a shorter distance (800m or 400m) and a longer distance (3000m/2 miles) once a month each. Each time you improve, you will set your sights on running a bit harder next time, and getting used to running faster laps. While you are racing regularly, I suggest that you do not increase the amount of training – in fact you may get a better result by doing only one hard training session in the week of a big race, and resting up for the last three days. If you have kept a record of your interval training, you will see that your average lap times are getting better.

A common discovery is that you get very good at running interval 400m laps, with a full lap recovery, but you cannot run anything like as fast as this in races. If this happens, cut your recovery jog down to a half-lap, taking not more than 2 minutes over it, and see how it feels. As you will be taking less time for the session, you can increase the number to two sets of five laps, or try doing the eight straight off, without the 5-minute rest between sets, and then work up to ten straight off. If you feel like making things a bit tougher, try doing the first two interval 400m with *no* interval – as a straight 800m. By this time you should be ready for the next level of training.

The 5-minute miler

In this range we might find widely different categories of people. The talented female distance runner is going to take around 4 minutes 40 for 1500m – in fact there are plenty of under-fifteen girls in the country who are close to this time. The young male athlete who has dabbled in all sorts of sports but never concentrated on running for very long will find that he can run a mile in 5 minutes, and then there are the enormous numbers of long distance runners, in their twenties, thirties and forties, for whom the 5 minutes 30 seconds mile is a common racing speed on the road, but who find it hard work to run a single mile in 5 minutes, and would like to increase their speed.

The following session is really for the first two categories, using a low mileage. The long distance men may like to take a holiday from their high mileage and try three months of speed training, or they may continue to run regular 10 to 15 mile distances, and just fit these speed sessions in on two days a week.

For the athlete who is already around 5 minutes for the mile or 4 minutes 40 for 1500m, we can assume a fairly high level of fitness and plunge straight into a pattern of interval training, repetition runs and speed work. When switching over to this pattern from a winter of cross-country and road, it is wise to introduce the fast sessions gradually. With my own athletes, we might put in the occasional track-type schedule on a fine day in February, then one a week in March, so that in April, which is holiday time for students, we can get a lot of good-quality training done.

The pattern which follows is something which might be done in late April, with one of the first races at the end of two weeks.

Schedule 19. Two-Week Training Cycle
(includes 3 to 4 rest days)

Day 1: 6 miles at a steady pace
Day 2: 2 miles warm-up, then 8 × 150m up a slope (1 in 20), 8 × 150m down the slope, 1 mile jog
Day 3: Warm-up, 10 × 400m in 72 to 73 seconds, with 200m recovery jog (2 to 2½ mins)
Day 4: 6 miles Fartlek
Day 5: Time-trial over a favourite course, roughly 1 to 2 miles, with long warm-up
Day 6: 6 miles steady, then 6 × 150m fast stride on grass
Day 7: Warm-up, 3 × 1000m approx. 5 minutes rest between each
Day 8: Fartlek run, 5 to 6 miles, with bursts on hills

Day 9: Warm-up, 8 to 10 × 300m, grass or track, starting at 54 seconds and getting faster. Keep to 2 minute recovery
Day 10: Race

The following is an example of the training done by Christine Benning in the late spring, preparing for the track season:

Schedule 20. Christine Benning's Spring Training

Sunday: 11 miles
Monday: Fartlek, A.M.; weights, plus 3-mile run, P.M.
Tuesday: 3 miles A.M.; track intervals, P.M.
Wednesday: 6 miles
Thursday: 4 miles, A.M.; track intervals, P.M.
Friday: 2 × 3 miles, A.M.; weights, plus 3-mile run, P.M.
Saturday: 3 to 4 × 1000m fast

There is no difference in principle between her training and that of a national class male runner. It is not surprising that Christine is one of the few British girl runners to have gone on improving consistently through her twenties. The Russian girls train up to 120 miles a week and go on improving into their late twenties, as do male distance runners.

Towards the 4-minute mile

The level of competition nowadays is such that any serious male middle distance runner has got to be running below 4 minutes for 1500m (4 minutes 18 for a mile) and below 1 minute 58 for 800m. With a solid background of winter training, including some cross-country races, along the lines suggested in Chapter 8, our ambitious runner will first of all be able to tackle a larger and faster version of the previous schedule. The numbers of intervals can be increased, if 1500m is the main aim, so that he is running two sets of 10 to 12 × 200m instead of 150m; the intervals over 400m will be speeded up to 67 to 68 seconds a lap, with a 2-minute recovery, and the times of the 1000m runs will come down. If 800m is the main aim, then one session a week will become faster, with longer recovery being allowed. Day 2 will become two sets of 6 × 200m in 30 to 32 seconds each, with a 2-minute recovery, and day 9 will become two sets of 4 to 5 × 300m, at your 800m speed or slightly faster.

The following schedule was designed for a runner aiming to run 1500m in around 3 minutes 50, and 800m in 1 minute 55. Once again, it is the kind of training which would be done in April in Britain, just before the competitive season gets under way. This particular session is designed for the 800m/1500m specialist, rather than for the 1500m/3000m runner.

Schedule 21. Two-Week Training Cycle for 800m/1500m Runner

WEEK 1

Sunday: 10-mile run, easy pace

Monday: 6 × 600m on grass, at 1500m speed (300m jog interval)

Tuesday: Fartlek run, 6 to 8 miles, bursts of 50m to 250m

Wednesday: 4 × 400m in 64 seconds (1½ minutes int.); 1 lap jog; 4 × 400m in 62 seconds (1½ minutes int.); 1 lap jog; 4 × 400m in 60 seconds

Thursday: On grass, untimed. 1 × 600m, 2 × 300m, 4 × 150m acceleration runs, 4 × 200m (pace changing)

Friday: Rest

Saturday: Club race or hard Fartlek session or fitness trial

WEEK 2

Sunday: 6-mile easy run, 2 to 3 miles of fast strides on grass

Monday: 10 × 200m, sub-30 seconds (50 seconds int.); 5 minutes rest; 10 × 200m, about 28 seconds (1 minute int.)

Tuesday: Run out to hills. 10 × 100m uphill, run back

Wednesday: 200m fast (200m jog int.); 400m fast (400m jog int.); 600m fast (600m jog int.); 400m fast (400m jog int.); 200m flat out. Jog down. Target times should be 30, 62, 93, 62 and sub-28 seconds

Thursday: Long warm-up. 1 × 400m (sub-55 seconds); 5 minutes rest. 4 × 200m striding, untimed

Friday: Rest or easy jog

Saturday: Race over 800m or 1500m. Go for fast-level pace

All interval sessions should be preceded by at least one mile of jogging, a thorough set of flexibility exercises, plus sit-ups, squat-thrusts and leg-raising exercises, and two laps of jogging and striding. Any intensive session should be followed by one mile of jogging.

Training at international level

The man or woman who reaches international level is not superhuman. Nobody springs on to the scene, fully-formed, as a 3 minutes 35 1500m runner. I have seen plenty of runners come through from good club or school level to the top national level. Some have become internationals, and some not. Of those who do make the national team, some have one season, win the British vest and disappear from the scene, while others establish themselves, and reappear year after year in the team, going to European, Commonwealth and Olympic Games. What makes them different? It may be just physical talent – people like Steve

Cram or Mary Decker have such an abundance of talent that all the coach has to do is point them in the right direction. However, the gap between the good club or school athlete and the international has now become so great that the right mental attitude is even more important than having the physical attributes. When it was possible to get into the British team by running 3 minutes 44 for 1500m, the talented young athlete, capable of, say, 3 minutes 52 at the age of nineteen, could see that he was only a couple of seasons away from international honours; but now we have runners in the 3 minutes 38 to 3 minutes 39 who are only on the fringe of international honours, and have little chance of a run in the big games meetings.

How can we motivate our talented youngsters to devote four or five years to really hard training, without the guarantee that they will make the highest level at the end of it? First, the thing is worth doing for its own sake. Nothing else, in my opinion, gives the same satisfaction as achieving a target for which you have trained and planned. By doing it, you have proved that you are the master of your own fate, that you *can* overcome difficulties. When you can handle hard training schedules and discipline yourself to carry them through, life's other problems become easier to handle.

In more specific terms, the athlete should have a short-term goal for each season – winning a county title, getting into a team, beating the qualifying time for the national championships. When you face a hard evening's training, after a day's work, dreams of making the Steve Ovett superstar class may be too distant to inspire you. It is better to fix your eyes on winning your Southern League race next week. The time for the big dreams and the big plans are when you review your year and plan the next step.

To make the highest level you are going to have to go into unknown territory, training more intensively than ever before. The prospect of training 50 or 60 miles a week may not bother you, but you will have to reach deep down inside yourself to put in that extra effort needed to rise from the 3 minutes 49 level to the 3.39 level, and you will have to do it several times a week in the hard training times.

You don't have to train hard twelve months of the year, in fact you will be better off if you don't. The processes by which the body improves itself are growth processes, and they will not take place if the body is under continued stress. There have got to be times within each week when you are resting, and there have got to be times in each year when you take the pressure off. I have been lucky to have been associated with Mike Boit, one of the greatest middle distance men of his day. Although two Olympic boycotts by the Kenyan team deprived him of the highest honour in his best years, his record is still remarkable; he won a bronze medal at 800m in the 1972 Olympics, and was placed fourth in the 1500m. He won a silver medal in the 1974 Commonwealth Games, a gold at 800m in 1978 and a bronze at 1500m in 1982. His records included a world record equalling 1 minute 43.6 seconds for 800m and an African record for the mile, of 3 minutes 49, set at the age of thirty-two. The following year, at thirty-three, he handed Steve Ovett a defeat at 1500m, clocking 3 minutes 34, and, at the time of writing, he is training for a place in the Los Angeles Olympics. How has he managed to do this, remaining in top class competition for thirteen years without having a serious injury? At the time when British runners are putting in 70 miles a week between November and January, Mike is running 10 to 15 miles a week. He may run a little in the indoor season, but he races seriously only from June to September, which means that he can concentrate on the other aspects of his life for the rest of the year.

In direct contrast to this, we have the eastern European pattern, which has been copied in some of the developing countries, of selecting a national squad and keeping them as full-time athletes, with big rewards for success. Which is the right way to follow? There is no doubt in my mind. The 'national squad' system may be the best for the country, but it is not the answer for the individual athlete. If you take the twenty best young athletes in Britain and put them in a training camp for six months, training hard against one another, you will probably destroy half of them. The ones who survive will be very tough, but they won't necessarily be medal-winners. This method selects the athletes who can best tolerate fifteen training sessions a week, not the ones who will win a 3½ minute race.

The Russians have had a well organized squad system for years. How many great Russian middle distance runners can you name? The ones you *can* name are all women. This is because the eastern European woman is culturally prepared to accept a high work load. In Britain and Australia the girl athletes do not seem prepared to make as many sacrifices for their sport as the men do. American girls, led by the great Mary Decker, are now training harder, and they will soon play a more prominent part in the world of middle distance running.

The right pattern for the western athlete is that set by Coe, Cram and Ovett. If you think that you have the talent, get a coach who can give you close personal attention, integrate your running life and your life of work and study, and be prepared to train very hard at certain times of the year.

Special aspects of middle distance training

It is not necessary for everyone to work on all these aspects at once, and some of them may not be necessary for some people.

Weight training. It cannot be coincidence that the best 800m/1500m men in the world are not only tall and long-legged, but they are usually well-developed in the upper body. Steve Scott and John Walker are classic examples. A generation before them, Herb Elliott and Peter Snell were the dominant figures. Both had good upper bodies. Peter Snell's build came naturally, Elliott developed his by swimming and weight training. Would he have been as great a runner without the weights? He and his coach, Percy Cerrutty, believed in the value of weights, and the improvement in strength gave him increased confidence. However, it is impossible to separate that benefit from the effect of the whole Cerrutty life-style, dedicated to really hard training in natural surroundings.

If you feel that you are deficient in upper body and/or leg strength, then you should find the effects of putting in a three-month period of weight training. For distance runners, who need to develop the blood supply along with the muscle fibres, I feel that the weight should be such as to allow you to do fifteen to twenty repetitions with each exercise, whereas sprinters, going for sheer power, will be using a much heavier weight and doing only six reps at a time. I also recommend long, slow running over the weight training period of the season, to develop the aerobic supply, and not much racing.

Flexibility and gymnastic work. There is still controversy here. A lot of young runners are now putting in an hour of flexibility work a day, mainly because Sebastian Coe does it. The argument in favour of flexibility is that it gives you a long, free-flowing stride. At that crucial moment when you start to bring your knee forwards and upwards, the muscles in your backside and underneath your thigh will tend to resist the stretching. If they can be made more flexible, the same amount of effort will give you a longer stride. In the same way, development of strength and flexibility in the foot and ankle must help your last bit of leg drive. Hopping and bounding exercises will help this, and they may also do something for the compressible or 'elastic' components of leg muscle, but nothing much is known of the training effects on these.

Against this, one can point out that there are a lot of men running under 3 minutes 35 for 1500m who have never spent any time on flexibility exercises, except for five minutes stretching in the warm-up. My own feeling is that if you have an extra half-hour a day to spare, it can do no harm, but the best training for running is running, and as long as you retain your natural flexibility by five minutes of exercises a day, there is nothing more to be gained. If you use resistance running in your training, such as running over soft sand, mud or thick grass, then you will develop the ankle strength at the same time as you are developing cardiovascular fitness.

Mental toughening. Mental strength is usually the thing that separates the champion from the merely good. It is not quite the same thing as competitive instinct. Mental strength is needed when things are going badly, and when you have to train hard in bad conditions. It can be increased by working in inspiring natural conditions. Herb Elliott used to say that his training was so tough that running four times round the track seemed easy. At least once a year you need to get right away from the track and train hard and long in mountains and forests. You must learn what it is like to run up and down mountain ridges until your body is crying out for rest, and then have to climb one more hill. You must acquire the confidence that your legs can carry you mile after mile, all day if necessary, over every sort of terrain. You must learn that you can endure extremes of weather, thirst, lack of sleep, boredom and discomfort, and still be the same person. If you can do all this, you will probably be a better runner and you will certainly be a better human being.

Specific event training. The world is full of people who can train for hours a day, but very few of them can run fast. Many runners shy away from the crucial high-pressure training which is needed to reach the highest level.

You must remember that you are training for an event which is all over in less than 2 minutes or 4 minutes. The prize goes to the man or woman who can concentrate every ounce of effort into those few moments. You have to run as if there was no tomorrow. Most of the year we are training through day after day, week after week, stressing the body, recuperating, building up and stressing again. In the competitive season the pattern is rest, explosive effort, recuperation, explosive effort, and so daily habits have to be changed.

In terms of training, this means that you run your interval training sessions in short sections, with only a small interval between the bursts. After a rest, you can repeat the dose. If you are doing repetitions, you are going as close as possible to racing conditions, and you may even try to simulate races by taking it in turns to play the role of front-runner and waiter. Training with Mike Boit in his early days, I knew that he was ready for a world-class performance when he ran two 800m in 1 minute 53, on a rough grass track, with only 4 minutes rest between them.

The hard runs have to be short, and run with total commitment. In between hard sessions and before races, you have to forget about serious training. The hard efforts will cause the accumulation of lactic acid in your legs, which may take 48 hours to disperse. The best way to recover is to jog gently for 4 to 5 miles, do a thorough set of stretching exercises and shower directly afterwards. Two easy runs a day, of 3 or 4 miles each, would be even better.

As an example of what might be done before a big race, this is the actual training done by Mike Boit before running 1 minute 43.7 seconds for 800m in Zurich in 1975.

Schedule 22. Mike Boit's 800m Training

Monday: A.M. Brisk 5-mile run
P.M. 6 × 400m, average 55.3 seconds (2 minutes recovery jog)
Tuesday: A.M. 5 miles steady
P.M. 5 × 500m, fast but not timed (200m jog interval)
Wednesday: A.M. jogging and striding on grass
P.M. 6 × 300m, av. 38.6 (about 3 minutes int.)
Thursday: P.M. 5 × 400m, av. 52.4 (3 minutes recovery)
Friday: P.M. 5 × 300m, av. 39.1 (about 4 minutes recovery)
Saturday: A.M. jogging on grass
P.M. 5 × 200m, standing start, av. 23.8 (4 minutes rest)
Sunday: P.M. 600 time-trial, standing start, 76.4 seconds
Monday: Rest
Tuesday: Easy jogging only
Wednesday: 800m race: 1 minute 43.7 seconds

All interval sessions preceded by 10 minutes warm-up plus flexibility exercises and followed by 30 minutes jogging.

For someone who has run, say, 3 minutes 45 for 1500m and is aiming to peak for national championships where he will hope to run 3.40, I would suggest the following preparation:

Schedule 23. Three-Week Countdown for 1500m Runner

TWO WEEKS BEFORE 3000m race

PENULTIMATE WEEK 1 day of 6 × 300m in 43 seconds, with a recovery jog of under 2 minutes; 1 day of 4 × 600m, 88 to 92 seconds, with 4 minutes rest between: other days, easy running.

FINAL WEEK
Saturday: 800m race
Sunday: Long easy run, 8 to 10 miles

Monday: 4 × 400m, 50 to 60 seconds (2 minutes jog), then 5 minutes rest and repeat 4 × 400m, 57 to 59 seconds
Tuesday: 4 miles easy
Wednesday: Long warm-up, then time-trial on 800 to 1000m grass circuit, plus 2-mile jog
Thursday: 4 to 6 mile easy run
Friday: 3-mile jog morning and evening
Saturday: A.M. 3-mile jog if evening race. P.M. Race

The time to push yourself really hard is in the penultimate week. In the final week you are really proving to yourself that the ability is there, so the two hard days will be at ninety-nine per cent effort. At the back of your mind is going to be the thought that Saturday is the day that counts, the day you will give it everything, the day when you will run as if there was no tomorrow.

10

The Long Distance Track Runner

This chapter covers all events from the 3000m/2 miles to the 10,000m/6 miles, including the 3000m steeplechase. The modern distance runner is faced with the quandary of which sphere of running to choose. Although the club runner can and does run cross-country, track and road, the top-class runner has to decide which is going to be his most important area, and make the others subservient to it. Men like Rose and Salazar, women like Mary Decker, are obviously going to win most of their races over most types of going, but even they have to make a choice if they want to be gold medallists or big prize-winners, because there are more and more runners competing at the higher levels.

Whether you take to the road or the country depends on your liking for mud, but choosing the track racing scene is something else. The track is not democratic, it is élitist. You don't go there so much for fun as to do battle with yourself and others, to prove what you can do. On the road, you can have a field of 500 in a 6-mile race, all running at their own speed, all achieving something, helping each other along, running to the best of their ability, but all having fun. The track is just not like that. There are winners, medallists and losers.

The track is mentally much tougher and more inhibiting than road or country. When I was competing there were many men around who were, frankly, better runners. In a straight race over 6 miles Ron Hill and Basil Heatley would always beat me, but on the track I could always beat them. Why? It is much more difficult to break contact in a track race, because there are no hills, no fences, no sharp corners.

The lap times tell you exactly how fast you are going and the lap scoring gives the countdown to the bell. The excitement and terror of the last lap cast a spell over the race, like the *dénouement* of a thriller. The suspense of waiting for the finish often paralyses the will of many a good runner. As he nears the finish he wonders: 'Have I got any kick left? Will I be able to sprint the whole of the last lap? What will happen if I can't drop them?'

The tactics of track racing are dealt with in the next chapter, but they tend to dominate both the choice of event and the training for it. The successful track runner has to be cool and calculating and he has to have a fair turn of speed. To run in the 1500m he has to be able to run the last lap in well under a minute, and even in the 5000m and the 10,000m last laps in 56 seconds are not uncommon. If he hasn't got this kind of speed, he has to be able to run much faster than the road runner over the last few laps of a race. The little Portuguese runner, Carlos Lopes, recently ran the last three laps of a 10,000m in 3 minutes 3 seconds.

To be snobbish about it, track is a lot classier than the other forms of running. It is like the Royal Ballet compared to a disco. For that reason, anyone who wants to be really good has got to apprentice himself as a track runner in his early years. When he has the skills, the speed, the ruthlessness of the successful track runner he may go on to the road and the country, with the knowledge that he has a better chance than most in the last stages of a race.

Basic 3000m/5000m training

Background training. Assuming that you are running in Britain, you are preparing for a season which runs from May to September. The necessary preconditioning will be two to three months, starting from a background of regular road running, if you want to get the best results. In the first four weeks you can follow the lines of my Jogger-into-

Runner schedule, if you feel that you are not fit enough to plunge straight into the programme which follows.

The emphasis is on variety, because we have to stress all the systems involved in running long and fast. We need strong legs, we need endurance at speed and we need to be able to change pace and to sprint. Because a lot of the useful work is done in the form of interval training, we need to find ways of making this constantly interesting and challenging.

Inevitably, there are regular sessions of training on the track itself, but in the early stages these should be only once every two weeks. If the British weather makes it impossible to get on to a track in February and March, you will have to use some other firm surface, and road will do if nothing else is available. In my early years I lived 60 miles from the nearest track, and did my intervals on a half-mile stretch of flat road measured with a bicycle wheel.

There are really two attitudes to distance running, which I call the 'German' and the 'Australian'. It is possible to succeed with either, but I like to try and blend them. The German method is based on interval training. The training is done on measured tracks, with the fast run and the recovery being timed. You know exactly where you are, but it can get very tedious training in the same venue all the time. The Australian method means getting out into wild surroundings and running hard over all sorts of going, but particularly over hills, on rough tracks and through sand dunes. The drawback to this is that, although it is very tough and challenging for a couple of weeks, you cannot be sure whether you are making progress. Being human, it is easy to go out at a good speed, put in a couple of good bursts in the first 2 miles, and then subside into a steady plodding sort of pace.

In my conditioning, I like to work on a fourteen-day cycle, with two easy days and two 'challenge' days. The latter may be races, a time-trial over one of my regular courses, or something like a mountain climb or a 20-mile run across Exmoor. On the other ten days I like to try to do ten different things, returning to each one every two weeks or so. In this way I have something to go for all the time. These ten will be as follows:

Schedule 24. Two-Week Preconditioning Programme
(excluding two rest/easy days and two challenge days)

Day 1: The long slow run, 13 miles or more, very slowly
Day 2: The medium pace run – for me, 8 to 10 miles over a regular, hilly course, timed.
Day 3: The short, fast run – 5 to 6 miles on road, timed
Day 4: Hill climbs
Day 5: Fartlek, 6 to 8 miles
Day 6: Cross-country or grass reps, about 900m to 1500m long
Day 7: Road reps, 1600m to 2400m long
Day 8: Resistance running (boots, sand or mud)
Day 9: Track intervals (10 to 20 × 400m)
Day 10: Road intervals

Apart from the long slow run, none of these sessions takes more than an hour to complete. If you are going to be a 5000m runner, you should get into the habit of doing 5000m of fast work in your interval and repetition sessions. If your cross-country circuit is about 1000m, or a little over 3 minutes running round the park, do five of those in a full session; if you are running on the road, the fast work should tot up to 15 or 16 minutes – say, 2 minutes fast, 2 minutes slow, then 6 × 1 minute fast, 1 minute slow, then 4 × 30 seconds fast, 1 minute slow.

The first time you go through this two-week cycle you will just be trying it out, not going 100 per cent at many of the sessions, but seeing whether or not you can handle the load. My kind of training will not suit everybody, because there are very few easy days. However, I hope that because they are all a little bit different, and place the stress on different things, there will always be one that you will be prepared to do. The exact order does not matter, but obviously it would be stupid to do all the interval and repetition sessions on four successive days. The hardest days, which are 4, 6, 7, 9 and 10, can be interspersed with days 1, 2, 3, 5 and 8. The two easy days, complete rest or a gentle 3 to 5 mile jog, will normally be before the two 'challenge' days.

The above programme is preconditioning for the track, rather than a training programme for the cross-country season, but if you look at Chapter 8 you will see that it resembles the Winter Training programme for those who are racing at that time of year. All you have to do is cut down on the hard training for the two days before your race.

Pre-season training. If you are following the preconditioning programme for eight to ten weeks, it will bring you to within four weeks of your first track race. In the last two-week cycle I suggest you have one track interval session a week, dropping the road intervals. There will have to be time for a speed session, too: running fast 200m stretches, working up to doing four to six really fast, and then easing off for the last two. This should not be done on a hard, i.e., all-weather, track because it will hurt your legs too much. An old type of cinder track will be all right, or firm level grass. Speed work has to be done on a good surface, because you have to train your muscles into a smooth balanced sprinting action. It is easy to see, at the start of a track season, those who have moved straight over from the cross-country, because they tend to roll like sailors, and their legs come 'round the side' instead of straight up and down.

Early season training. The following schedule was designed for someone running 5000m and 3000m, hoping to get down to 14 minutes 45 for 5000m and 8 minutes 40 for 3000m. It is a tough schedule, with a lot of interval training, and the beginner should substitute an easy run, or Fartlek on grass, for one of the weekly interval sessions.

Schedule 25. Two-Week Programme for 3000m/5000m Runner

WEEK 1

Sunday: 10-mile run, easy pace
Monday: 8 to 10 × 600m, on grass, at 3000m speed
Tuesday: Fartlek run, 6 to 8 miles, doing 1 minute fast, 1 minute slow
Wednesday: 15 × 400m, averaging 69 (1½ minutes int.)
Thursday: 10 × 200m on grass, 30–31 speed (40 seconds int.); 5 minutes rest; repeat 10 × 200m
Friday: 3 miles easy jog
Saturday: Warm-up. Club races or 3 × 1 mile repetition (6 minutes int.)

WEEK 2

Sunday: 6 miles cross-country. 2 to 3 miles of striding on grass
Monday: 4 × 800m, 2.18 (400m jog int.), 4 × 400m, 67–68 seconds (200m jog int.), 4 × 200m stride
Tuesday: Run out to hills. 10 × 100m uphill. Run back
Wednesday: 7 × 600m on grass or 10 to 12 × 400m, 65 to 66 seconds (200m jog int.)
Thursday: 1 × 800m, 2.16, 5 minutes rest; 1 × 400m, 60 seconds, 8 × 200m stride
Friday: Rest
Saturday: 3000m or 5000m race

All interval sessions should be preceded by at least one

mile of jogging, a thorough set of flexibility exercises, plus sit-ups, squat-thrusts and leg raising exercises, and two laps of jogging and striding. Any intensive session should be followed by one mile of jogging.

The 3000m runner. A lot of runners will be trying to spread themselves over a wide range of events, running 1500m or 5000m for their club in league races, or possibly 3000m steeplechase; if they are in their early twenties, their distance-running potential is probably best revealed by the time they can run over 3000m. At the same time, they will want to improve their basic speed and their times over 800m and 1500m. The following schedule is designed for this type of person:

Schedule 26. Two-Week Programme for 3000m Runner

WEEK 1

Sunday: Long easy run, strides on grass

Monday: 5000m session: 4 to 5 × 800m at faster than 5000m speed, then 5 × 400m, slightly faster than the 800s

Tuesday: Easy running, 5 to 7 miles

Wednesday: 1500m session: three sets of 4 × 400m, with 200m jog in 2 minutes between each run, and an extra 3 minutes rest between sets. The first set of 400s are slower than 1500m speed, and the average speed of each set should get faster, e.g., 66, 64, 62

Thursday: Fartlek run, including hills or sand dunes

Friday: Rest or easy run

Saturday: Minor race

WEEK 2

Sunday: Long easy run, plus several fast 200m on grass

Monday: 3000m session: 4 × 600m on grass (2 minutes recovery), 4 × 300m in 47 to 48 seconds (1½ minutes recovery)

Tuesday: Easy running, 5 to 7 miles
Wednesday: 800m session: 4 × 150m fast stride, 3 to 4 × 400m, sub-60 seconds (3 minutes recovery), 4 × 200m, 27 to 29 seconds (2 minutes recovery)
Thursday: 4 to 6 miles steady, a few strides
Friday: Rest
Saturday: Race

Steeplechasing. Obviously the steeplechaser is a distance runner, since his event goes on for about 9 minutes, but other qualities are needed. Apart from being able to hurdle, he must have the mental and physical ability to withstand the constant breaks in rhythm. Because of the constant change in pace, the oxygen demand per minute is greater than in flat running, and there is more stress on the anaerobic systems. The steeplechaser has to be strong in the legs, flexible in the hips and he has to have the qualities of a good 1500m runner. Few really good runners turn to the steeplechase, because it is less frequently run, but when they do, it is more often the good 1500m runner who has the greater success, as compared with the good 5000m runner. Kipchoge Keino and Filbert Bayi, in spite of their poor technique over the barriers, won gold and silver medals in the Olympics when they turned to the steeplechase. Neither had regular racing experience in the event, but the qualities which made them great 1500m runners suited them for the longer distance too.

Training for the steeplechase is going to differ from the 3000m programme given above only in including hurdling. The would-be steeplechaser must do the hurdler's flexibility exercises every day, starting in the conditioning period. During the pre-competitive period, one interval session a week should be done over barriers, including the water-jump if you have one available. This session can be either the 3000m or the 1500m session given in the above schedule. Apart from this, the steeplechaser has to make hurdling second nature. There was a story about Bruce Jenner, the Olympic decathlon winner, that he had a hurdle in his living-room, which he had to hurdle every time he went in or out of the door! I don't recommend putting a steeplechase barrier in your living-room, but I hope you take the point.

If you have no proper barrier available, use an ordinary hurdle and set it at 3 feet high (92.5cm), or make your own. Have this available in the place where you normally do your warming-up, so that when you have done your usual jogging and stretching, you can put in several runs over the hurdle.

Hurdling technique cannot be learned from books. If you want to do it seriously, find someone at your local athletic club or school who can demonstrate hurdling to you, and practise, practise, practise. Don't worry too much if your hurdling style is poor. As long as it is not too wasteful of energy, hurdling style matters less in the steeplechase than physical fitness and mental drive. Amos Biwott won the Olympic title in 1968 with the worst technique ever seen. His success was due partly to his ability to cope with the altitude and partly to his incredible competitive drive, which enabled him to come bounding through in the latter part of the race, when everyone else was giving up. The great steeplechaser is the man who can attack before and after every hurdle, and rise from the dead after every water-jump.

The 10,000m runner

When I was competing, this event used to be a sort of consolation race for ageing runners who couldn't make international level at anything shorter. If you could produce a last lap in something approaching 60 seconds you were bound to win. Such is no longer the case. The

10,000m man has got to have the full armoury of tactical weapons, including a sprint finish, and he has got to be able to withstand the tedium of going twenty-five times around the track. It is not so much the pace which gets you, as that feeling that it is never going to end. When you have run ten laps you are nearly at the end of a 5000m, but if it is a 10km you still have fifteen laps to go! As in a marathon, you have to think of the first half as a mere preliminary, before the real race gets going. During this part you are going to switch to 'automatic pilot' and try to use as little mental energy as possible. You try to stay out of trouble, avoid leading, minimize changes of pace and just run relaxed, but in touch with the leaders. This means that in training you have got to get used to clocking up the repetition miles at your racing speed.

Winter training for the 10,000m man is going to be on the same lines as for the 5000m, but as he probably started off running shorter track distances, he is going to increase his winter mileage over previous years. Sixty to 80 miles a week will be necessary to perform at top level, so you are approaching the training volume of the average marathon runner. When I was training seriously for the 10km I found that I could match the best road runners over any distance up to 20 miles. I never tried the marathon distance at that time, but I always feel that my time of 1 hour 41 minutes for 20 miles, done on 65 miles a week training, was a very good argument for the quality system of training as opposed to mere quantity.

In the pre-competitive and early season phases, you must work up to doing 10,000m or more of fast work in your hardest sessions. Your repetition sessions will become 8 to 10 × 100m and 4 to 5 × 1½ miles. In your interval training you have got to get used to twenty-five laps. I found that a good way to get through them was to do 8 × 800m first, and then switch to single 400m laps. It sounds a lot? Emil

Zátopek was doing 30 × 400m back in the 1950s, and he once did a session of 40 × 400m.

If you look at the sessions of leading 5000m, 10,000m and marathon runners, you will find a lot of similarity. The marathon runners have got to include fast work, and the track runners have got to do high mileage if they are going to cope with running several races in a short space of time.

This is an example of Brendan Foster's training in early April, when he was building up for the Olympic 10,000m in Montreal the following summer (he was Britain's only medal-winner on the track in those games).

Schedule 27. Brendan Foster's 1976 Olympic 10,000m Training

Sunday: 20 miles easy
Monday: A.M. 10 miles steady
P.M. 10 miles hard
Tuesday: A.M. 10 miles steady
P.M. 10 miles steady, with three hard stretches
Wednesday: A.M. 10 miles steady. Very tired
P.M. 10 miles steady. Very tired indeed
Thursday: A.M. 10 miles steady
P.M. 10 miles steady. Going well but very tired
Friday: A.M. 5 miles steady
P.M. 5 miles steady
P.M. (evening) 5 miles steady
Saturday: A.M. Intervals on the track, 10 × 400m, average 61.3, with 90 seconds rest between
P.M. 10 miles steady
Total mileage: 131

The sheer volume of this training, which was not the biggest week, is sufficient for any marathon man, and the speed of the interval training is that of a good 1500m runner. While admiring his courage and dedication, it is my view that a more varied programme, with a little more rest, would have produced just as good results and would have been more fun. However, you cannot disentangle the training from the personality. Because Brendan Foster had the tenacity to pursue such a programme, he was Britain's most successful international competitor on the track from the early 1970s until his retirement.

Training in the competitive season

The long distance track man becomes a compulsive trainer. Often the hardest thing for him is learning to rest up properly before races. His life is organized into a pattern of 'train, eat, work, train, eat, sleep' and at crucial times the pattern is altered.

Hard training depletes the glycogen reserves and causes accumulation of lactic acid in the blood. It may take two or three days for things to return to normal after a hard session, and during the hardest part of the year's training the runner may feel almost permanently tired. Unless he can adjust his resting and training pattern at the right time, all this effort will be wasted.

A look at Chapter 6 will show you the pattern of rest preceding a marathon. The pattern in the penultimate week before a big track race should be the same, alternating hard and easy days. In the last week you should resist the temptation to put in a long hard session and restrict yourself to no more than 15 minutes of hard effort on the Monday and Wednesday before a Saturday race. There is no reason why you should not continue to run easily every day, because it will help to maintain your normal patterns of eating and sleeping, and if you are travelling to a meeting, a run when you get there will help you to get over the journey. These runs *must* be easy, though, if you are to get the full benefit of the training of the previous weeks.

You must prepare mentally, by thinking over the way

you are going to run your race. I am a great believer in positive thinking. If you go over the possible ways the race might be run, and visualize yourself coming out successfully in each situation, you convince yourself that you cannot be beaten. When the race gets tough, as all races do sooner or later, it's the man who hasn't visualized himself winning who is most likely to quit. The man who is determined to win, who sees himself winning, won't quit until he is really at the end of his tether. Emil Zátopek once said: 'When I am feeling tired, I know the others must be tired too. If they weren't tired, they would be ahead of me. So, when I feel tired, I attack, and when I feel really tired, I sprint!' Zátopek, as well as being a tough competitor, has a sense of humour.

Here is an example of Brendan Foster's training, a few weeks before he demolished the European 5000m field in Rome in 1974:

Schedule 28. Brendan Foster's 1974 European 5000m Training

Sunday: 20 miles steady
Monday: A.M. 10 miles steady run to work
P.M. 8 miles steady
Tuesday: A.M. 5 miles steady
P.M. 5 miles steady
P.M. (evening) Track repetitions, 3 × 800m, average 2.01.3 with 4 to 4½ minutes rest. Very hard. 4× 100m on grass
Wednesday: A.M. 9 miles steady to work
P.M. Intervals. Two sets of 8 × 200m, with 20 seconds rest between, plus 4 × 100m
Thursday: A.M. 6 miles steady
P.M. 5 miles steady
P.M. (evening) 5 miles steady

Friday: A.M. 6 miles steady to work
P.M. GB v Czechoslovakia, 1500m. 1st in 3.41.2
Saturday: 15 miles quite fast
Total mileage: 110
Sunday: A.M. Track repetitions, 3 × 1 mile, av. 4 minutes 10 seconds (very hard)
P.M. 10 miles steady. Very tired

By contrast, here is an example of my training in May 1966, a few weeks before I broke the British 6-mile record:

Schedule 29. Bruce Tulloh's 1966 6-mile Training

Sunday: 6 miles easy on grass (slight leg strain)
Monday: A. M. 4-mile jog
P.M. Repetitions on grass. 8 × 1100m, average 3.14 (2 minutes jog)
Tuesday: A.M. Speed work. 8 × 100m stride, 5 × 100m sprint, then jog
P.M. Intervals, 20 × 400m av. 66.4 on grass (50 seconds int.)
Wednesday: 5 miles easy Fartlek
Thursday: Club race. 1 mile 4.18m, 400m relay leg (rough grass track)
Friday: A.M. 2-mile jog
P.M. 4 miles easy Fartlek
Saturday: Intervals. 24 × 300m, 47 seconds approx. (45 seconds jog int.)
Total mileage: 57

What conclusions can one draw? First of all, Brendan Foster was putting in far more miles a week, mostly 'steady running', which means far more slowly than his 5000m racing speed. Out of his fourteen sessions, eleven were long aerobic sessions, two were fast, intensive, largely anaerobic sessions, and one was a short race. Of my ten outings, three were fairly slow, four were around racing-speed, so were partly aerobic, partly anaerobic, and three were mostly anaerobic. Which is best? Foster's training certainly produced far better results – on that type of training he produced times in 1974 of 3 minutes 37 for 1500m, 13 minutes 14 for 5000m and 27 minutes 45 for 10,000m (27.33 three years later). My equivalent times were 3 minutes 42, 13 minutes 40 and 28 minutes 23. Moreover, the increased mileage of the modern runner enables him to recover more quickly from hard races, which is essential for the man who needs to be able to race in Nice, London, Rome and Helsinki within the space of eight days. However, the figures can be used to argue in different ways. First, the runner who has yet to break 14 minutes 30 for 5000m and 30 minutes for 10,000m might be better off doing the 'Tulloh' type of training, and then moving up to the 'Foster' level of work when he feels the need. If you are doing 110 miles a week at the age of nineteen and not running very fast or competing very successfully you may wonder whether the effort is worthwhile. My methods enabled me to run times which are still faster than many of the 100-mile-a-week brigade today, and the time needed does enable one to lead a normal life.

There are other valid points to be made. One could say: 'Suppose Tulloh, who obviously had ability, had done the kind of mileage in the 1960s that Foster was doing in the 1970s, would he not have been a lot better?' The answer is probably: 'Yes, he would.' However, that is hindsight, and at the time one tends to stick with the method that is successful. One could equally say: 'If Tulloh's methods enabled him to be the best in Britain and Europe on 50 miles a week, could they not be applied to give even better results on the "Foster" level of effort?' The answer is again: 'Yes, they could.'

Each runner is his own experiment. The training distances and the intensity of training he selects often depend more on his temperament and his opportunities than on what is really best for him. If we had a runner with the talent of, say, Steve Cram, and the dedication of Brendan Foster, who was not forced to get his training done by running to and from work, what sort of programme would I recommend? The ideal combination would be to maintain the daily mileage at 15 and 20 miles a day, with time allowed for rest and massage after each session. This would enable a higher proportion of good quality, race-related sessions to be done, without losing out on the occasional intensive anaerobic sessions. This is the kind of training which will have to be done by the person who is going to run 5000m in 12 minutes 50 and the 10,000m in 27 minutes.

Schedule 30. The '1990' Training Programme

Sunday: A.M. 20 miles, mostly steady, with a few fast single miles during the second half
P.M. 6 miles on grass, with 12 × 150m fast stride
Monday: A.M. 8 miles steady
P.M. Repetitions. 10 × 1km in 2.45 (2 minutes int.), on grass or sand
Tuesday: A.M. 8 miles steady
P.M. 10 to 12 miles, good speed, with bursts and surges
Wednesday: A.M. 8 miles easy on grass
P.M. Intervals on track. 8 × 800m average 2.07 (2 minutes int.), 5 minutes rest, then 10 × 400m, 61 to 63 (1 minute int.)
Thursday: A.M. 8 miles easy
P.M. Intervals. 3 sets of 10 × 250m fast stride (30 seconds int.)

Friday: A.M. 5 miles steady
P.M. Warm-up, then 5 miles hard on road
P.M. (evening) 5 miles easy Fartlek
Saturday: A.M. 5 miles easy
P.M. Road race or club track races, e.g., 1500m 3.49, 5000m aiming at 13.30, 400m relay leg
Total mileage: 120 approx.

This is probably not the limit. Dave Bedford got up to 200 miles a week in training, and ultra-distance runners can maintain 50 to 60 miles a day of steady plodding for weeks on end, which is around 400 miles a week. However, the crucial part of training takes place during the recovery phase, both during the training session and after it. With the correct use of massage and rest, and with a good diet, it should be possible to do three useful sessions a day. However, fatigue must be your guideline. If you are tired when you start training, and if this happens three days in a row, it is a sign that you need more rest. If you ignore the body's warning signs, you are going to break down, and then all the effort you have put in is wasted. You are worse off than if you had just done very light training.

As training and competition moves towards higher and higher standards, the best runner is the one who has the health to absorb these huge training loads. The ambitious long distance runner has got to move steadily upwards, year by year. The target for the 10,000m man, or the road racer, should be to work up to 120 miles a week by his mid-twenties. If the ambitious eighteen-year-old is doing 50 miles a week, then an increase in weekly mileage of only 10 miles a week each year, without sacrificing the quality of the training, will enable this target to be met.

11
Track Tactics

With good tactics you may be able to beat someone who is physically better than you. If you are better than everyone else you will probably win whatever tactics you use – that is the purpose of training hard – but if you are running against people who are physically as good as you and maybe better, you will need tactics. It is very often a matter of bluff. If you can convince the rest of the field that they cannot beat you, they will give up. If you are really out to win, you have to carry your tactical moves through with total conviction, right up to the last possible moment before you yourself crack up. If getting second or third means something to you, you may have to compromise your tactics, and this must be thought out before the race. Thus, if there are three places going in a team, but two of the places have already been allocated, you have got to run to win at all costs; if getting in the first three is what really matters, your plans may be different.

There are really only two tactical plans – that of the front-runner and that of the follower or waiter. The follower will, of course, hope to take the lead at some point, and when he does so he assumes the role of the front-runner.

Front-running. The front-runner is trying to impose his own personality – he is trying to establish mental and physical domination over the rest of the field. When he takes the lead he is throwing down a challenge and he is establishing himself as a person who is hoping to win the race. It is physiologically most economical to start off at level pace, but the front runner usually starts at a faster-than-average speed to frighten the others, and to make them run his pattern of race. They will immediately start worrying about whether they can keep up this pace, and by making them worry he is already part of the way towards his objective.

The longer the race, the more effective the front-runner's tactic becomes, because he has more time to test out the mental strength of his opponents. The most famous, and the most successful, front-runners have all been 10,000m men – Zátopek, Kuts, Nurmi, Clarke, Bedford. The first three were usually superior to the men they ran against – though not when they started their careers; the latter two had some great wins and ran world records from the front, but in Olympic competition they found that there were men of equal calibre, who would not succumb in the same way as the majority. The front-runner must realize that in a top-class field he has very little chance of breaking away from the pack in the first half of the race. The race only gets going after halfway, perhaps in the last third of the race, and in the early part he is just softening them up for the big punch.

Variation of pace, handled in the right way, is the front-runner's best weapon. Vladimir Kuts, and, more recently, Henry Rono, were the best at this, putting in bursts over and over again, until their opponents just gave up. The classic race was that of Kuts against Gordon Pirie in the Melbourne Olympics. Kuts put in tremendous variations of pace, and the two of them were nearly half a lap ahead of the field at one point, but whatever he did, Pirie hung on. They went through the 4 mile and 5 mile points in world record times, then, in the twenty-first lap, Kuts came almost to a standstill, so that Pirie was forced to lead. Having watched Pirie for 100m, Kuts put in one more hard burst, and Pirie cracked completely. A lesser man than Pirie would have settled for the silver medal, but for him it was gold or nothing. The Russians later told him that if Pirie had been able to resist that last burst, Kuts would have dropped out. The world has never seen a harder competitor than Vladimir Kuts; he had the strength to keep his tactical plan going to the last drop of his endurance.

Without having to go to these lengths, it is often possible to use local conditions to help you. The vital thing is breaking contact, and there is usually some point on the lap where conditions change – a loose patch on a cinder track, a head wind or a sunny side of the track. If you can put in a burst just before this point, the follower suddenly finds himself facing this difficult patch on his own; he falters briefly, and the leader has broken away.

The waiter's tactics. The problem here is that the majority of runners in a track race are playing the waiting game, and what may enable you to beat the front-runner may also be the right pace for someone else to beat you. If the front-runner sets a very fast pace, the tactics are simple; you just have to hang on, smooth out the pace as much as possible, and make your challenge at the last possible moment. If the pace is comfortable enough for a group of runners to stay in touch with the leader, the decision you make depends on your basic speed. If you have the capacity to accelerate quickly and can sprint fast over 50 yards, you leave your effort until the finishing straight. The Italian, Cova, is the expert at this. If you are feeling fresh and are confident of maintaining your speed, you can make your move just before the final bend, with about 200m to go, as Eamonn Coghlan did in the 5000m in the 1983 World Championships. This has the advantage of forcing the men behind you to run wide in order to stay in touch with you, or risk losing contact.

If you are not the fastest kicker in the field, you are forced to rely on the 'tactical jump', which must take place not later than 300m from the finish. If you kick with 300m to go, in all but the slowest races, you have long enough to exhaust everyone's strength. You will gain a couple of yards by kicking first, and a couple of yards is quite a lot to make up if the finishing speed is really fast. You cannot do it, though, unless you yourself have developed a great anaerobic capacity. This means that you must be a fast 400m runner, able to run close to 50 seconds (for a man) or 55 seconds (for a woman). If you lack that capacity, you have got to turn the finish of your distance race into the kind of middle distance race which suits you best. This may mean kicking with two, three or four laps to go.

At whatever stage you kick, it must be done with commitment, even if it is only a bluff – *particularly* if it is a bluff. Say you are in a group of four, and only the first two are going to get selected for the national championships. The leader is a front-runner whom you can out-kick, but the other two guys are pretty fast. If you put in a really fast lap with three laps still to run, you have a good chance of dropping at least one of the others. You may not be able to keep this pace going to the end, but he is not to know that. Once he has dropped, he is not likely to come back, and the longer you can maintain your burst, the better your chances of getting clear. Of course, by taking over the role of the front-runner, you slightly weaken your chances of winning if one of the others keeps his head and uses you as a pace-setter, but even if you do get beaten, you have given yourself the maximum chance of making the first two, because you have run as hard as you can.

Beating the waiter. There are more ways than one of killing a cat. If you are not a fast finisher, you have obviously got to run the race as fast as possible, but tearing off at a terrific pace is not the best way to do it. Unless the opposition are very inexperienced, they will realize that you can't keep up the pace, and as you slow they will close on you, and having run at a level pace, they will be fresher than you. On the other hand, setting off at an exactly level pace to run the best time you are capable of is not right either. You are merely acting like a mechanical hare and the rest of the field will say 'thanks very much' and use your efforts to help them to a good time too.

The front-runner cannot expect to break away until halfway through the race at least. In the early stages he might just as well save his energy and run at a level pace, but then he should start pushing the pace up, stretching the muscles and the minds of his opponents, while keeping them guessing about how much he still has left. The best piece of front-running in modern times was Brendan Foster's win in the European 5000m in Rome in 1974. The weather was extremely hot, and the early pace was not very fast, but in the eighth lap Brendan just took off, putting in a 400m burst in around 60 seconds and then maintaining a fast tempo for several more laps so that no one had a chance of closing the gap. Almost as impressive was Henry Rono's win in the Commonwealth Games 10,000m in 1978. As the world record-holder, he had a psychological advantage, which he exploited by playing the field, and treating the race as a Fartlek session. He would stride away down the straights and then ease up round the bends. Sometimes he would keep the pressure up for 200m, sometimes for only 50m, and when he really applied the pressure the rest of the field no longer had any thought of being able to win.

The ultimate in front-running tactics was shown by Mary Decker, who was able to lead the powerful Russians for the entire race in the 1983 World Championships 3000m and still outsprint them in the home straight.

Front-running counter-tactics. It is easier to be a follower. In terms of pure physical effort, the front-runner faces more air resistance than the man running just behind him.

This becomes less of a disadvantage in longer races as the pace is slower, but in a strong wind it will make a lot of difference, whatever the distance. It is also easier psychologically, because as long as you stay in contact, your tactical plan is working, whereas the leader's tactical plan is not working. You don't have to worry about whether you are going fast enough, as long as you are in touch.

The disadvantage is that you cannot run at the pace which suits you best, but have to follow that set by the leader, even though it may be uneconomically fast. If you use your head you can make this work to your advantage, by 'smoothing out' the pace and remaining in contact. Let us say that you are lapping at 68 seconds a lap, which is pretty close to the fastest pace at which you can keep going without the lactic acid building up. The leader puts in a fast 100m burst, speeding up to a 64-second speed. He therefore runs the 100m of that burst in 16 seconds, carries on with the next 100m in 17 seconds, but is then forced to slow down to 18 seconds for the 100m, because of the effort of the burst. If the follower is clever enough, he can allow the leader to gain 5 yards during the burst and then pull them back in the next 200m without making any additional effort. He will then close up on the leader, moving at a slightly faster pace, and can afford to move right up on to his shoulder, showing him that the burst has been totally ineffective.

In a modern distance race the finish may extend over four laps. When I was running 10,000m I used to think of the last mile as the time to stretch out and go for home. You can do this in two ways, either by gradually accelerating, winding up the pace lap by lap and straight by straight, or you can put in a tactical jump, break contact and go it alone. The latter step needs the greatest will-power, because you have exposed yourself and the opposition know that if they can catch you they will probably beat you; but if you are running to win, rather than just to place, the tactical jump gives you the best chance. If you break away with four laps to go, you have got to keep the pressure up with three to go. If you are still clear with two laps to go, the chances of success should give you enough lift to keep you going. You have to tell yourself that the others must be feeling worse than you are, otherwise they wouldn't have let you go.

Mental strength. In a championship final, everyone there is good. The race goes to the man who is not only physically strong, but who is convinced in his own mind that he should win and that he is going to win. Even if you are not the fastest man in the field, you can convince yourself that this is the day when everything is going to come right. Olympic history shines with examples of men and women who refused to accept defeat, who refused to accept that they had no chance. Some men who have run very fast times just cannot reproduce them under the pressure of a championship race. Others, who may have been only the second- or third-string men in their team, find that the excitement of running in a big race brings out the best in them. Harry Wilson, Steve Ovett's coach, once said that he tells his athletes to look on big races as *opportunities*, not as ordeals. This is the right attitude. You have months of training behind you – this is your chance to show what you can do. You will have a plan however vague and flexible when you come to the race. Once you go into the race you must make every effort to put your plan into operation. Time after time, even at Olympic level, you see athletes running with effort to put themselves in a winning position. They may have had a plan when they started, but you can see that after a lap or two they have decided just to stay in touch and see what happens at the finish. Eamonn Coghlan has the best competitive record on indoor tracks of anyone in his generation; he is very strong physically, he has excellent pace judgement and he is a very fast miler. In spite of this, he has twice thrown away the chance of an Olympic medal, finishing fourth in the 1500m in 1976 and in the 5000m in 1980. He was in the right position, and he had, in theory, more finishing power than anyone else there, but he was not convinced that he was going to win. In Montreal (1976) he was up against John Walker and in Moscow Miruts Yifter. Neither of these was infallible; they lost many other races at other times, but they shared the quality of total belief in themselves on the day that really mattered. Coghlan's win in the 1983 World Championships was a triumph of self-mastery as much as of physical ability.

800m. In world record races, the pace is getting closer and closer to even pace throughout. This is because the pace itself is so fast – just over 50 seconds per lap – that the runners are going into oxygen debt very rapidly, and the lactic acid is building up all the time. Any increase in this pace will lead to an even faster build-up of lactic acid, which will slow them down. The 1 minute 40 seconds 800m, which will come before the end of this century, will have to be run with each 200m section completed in very close to 25 seconds.

For ordinary mortals the race is further away from an all-out sprint. It is more aerobic, depending partly on how much oxygen you can take in during the race. It seems to make less difference to the eventual time if the first lap is 2 or 3 seconds faster than the next one. For tactical reasons, everyone starts fast in order not to get left at the back of the field, and the surge of adrenalin allows you to run a fast first lap before the pain catches up. Somebody hoping to run a 1 minute 58 would probably hope for a first lap time of 58 seconds, and somebody hoping for a 1.50 would want to go through in 54 seconds.

In a fast race it does not really matter if you are at the back of the field, because you will probably be running closer to level pace and as the field will be strung out in single file you will not have to run much extra distance to pass. You will avoid getting knocked about in the initial rush, too. However, if the race is slow or medium paced, the men or women at the back are at a severe disadvantage. They may be 10m behind the leader. They either have to run extra distance around the top bend to keep in touch, or they will have to make up over 10m in the last 300m. If the leader is sprinting at a speed of 27 seconds for the last 200m, the back-markers will have to run close to 25 seconds to win.

If you are hoping to win, you have to be in the first four places at the bell – what you do before that hardly matters. You may have to run outside somebody to keep your position, but if you are on the outside of the fast lane it won't matter too much, and it is probably better than being boxed in in third or fourth place if the race is slow. Running in the outer part of lane two is wasteful. All tracks nowadays have a long finishing straight, and you have time to get off the bend and make your effort up the straight. A lot of tension is generated and energy wasted by attacking while running wide around the bottom bend. It is crazy to throw away 3m in the last 200m when you are running flat out. The only people who should be running wide are those who are placed sixth, seventh and eighth, if they are hoping to place in the first three. Having economized on the first lap, or simply been shoved to the back, they may be a little bit fresher. Unless they can close up to within 3m of the leaders they will have no chance of getting to the front in the last 80m. In an ordinary sort of race there will probably be a big difference in ability between the winner and the eighth man, but in a championships final, every man is a potential medallist.

The ideal place to be in an 800m is in second place, on the shoulder of the leader, so that you can react to anyone trying to come past you. If you run in third place, on the inside, you will get maximum protection from the wind and run the shortest distance, but you will probably be boxed in by the second and fourth men running outside you. You will have to rely on luck and a bit of aggression to be able to attack the leader at some point in the last 300m. The leader will often move out towards the second lane as he comes out of the final bend. This forces the men who are trying to overtake him to run even further, but it leaves a gap on the inside, and Olympic titles have been won by the third placed man stealing through that gap while the leader is fighting a battle with the man outside him.

1500m and the mile. The same general principles apply here as to all distance races, but because the race is so much shorter than the 5000m, the runners are going to be more bunched, and some of the 800m tactics apply. The first 200m go with a rush, as everyone tries to establish himself in the first four places, but the next two laps are likely to be extremely tactical, before the pace starts hotting up for the finish. If you are one of the best runners in the field it will be worth your while starting to put on the pressure before the last lap sprint, because this will discourage the weaker members from getting ideas, and it will increase your chances of getting a place. It need not decrease your chances of winning, as long as you know what you are doing. You are controlling the race from the front, not running flat out but ready for an attack at any time after the bell.

If you are mentally strong, there is no reason why you should not lead all the way and win. The Kenyans have done this successfully at 800m and Filbert Bayi succeeded in beating John Walker this way in the Commonwealth Games 1500m. However, the front-running will more usually be done by someone who feels that he has little chance of winning but would rather lose in a fast time than a slow time. His attitude is: 'If you are going to beat me, you are going to have to run damned hard to do it.' Such an attitude can bring surprising results. The other runners in the field may be a little tired, if they have run heats the previous day, and they may be psychologically ready to fight out the last 400m, but not prepared for a race that is fast the whole way. This is where the 1500m/5000m runner can sometimes outlast the specialists.

The essential quality in winning at this distance, apart from sheer fitness, is mental agility. You may have to deal with a fast pace from the gun, or a terrific increase in speed from 700m out, or a sudden kick at any time in the last lap. The successful competitor has to use all his senses to be aware of what the others are doing. The rabbit is a much maligned animal, but its peripheral vision is so good that it can see predators coming up behind it and put in a quick burst before they pounce. Frightened rabbits win a lot of races.

All runners need 'stickability', but it is of paramount important at this distance. In a longer race, if the other guy is fitter, he is going to drop you anyway, but in a 1500m the race is soon over, and even if you think you cannot maintain the pace, you must have the confidence to go with the man who makes the break. Very often it will be a desperate gamble on his part. For a brief moment he has a surge of adrenalin. He hits the front, going as fast as he can, hoping to burn everyone off. If you can stay with him for another 20m his confidence may go, then his stride will shorten or he will tense up. Then it is your turn. When you hit the front, don't think of the opposition, think of your own action and try to keep up a fast rate of striking and a smooth action all the way to the finish. A bad runner will often roll and grimace and tighten his neck muscles when passed, as if to say: 'You can't blame me for being beaten; can't you see I'm trying as hard as I can?' The good runner will try to keep his form *and* run as hard as he can, until he has crossed the finishing line. In the 1983 World Championships it was significant that Steve Cram and Steve Scott, who placed first and second, were always alert to cover a break, whereas Ovett was not.

5000m and 10,000m. As in the shorter distances, the faster the pace, the closer it will be to level pace. A steady pace of 66 seconds per lap gives 2 minutes 45 per kilometre, level pace for a 13 minutes 45 5000m or a 27 minutes 30 10,000m. At club level, 72 seconds a lap gives 3 minutes per kilometre, the right pace for a 15 minute 5000m or a 30 minute 10,000. Variations from that pace are going to be costly, and so it is advisable to keep close to level pace in the first half of the race, unless you really like being out in front. If you are one of the weaker members of the field, it is in your interests to keep the pace going if it falls below your personal best speed. Getting beaten in slow races is not going to make you a better runner – you will learn a lot more by getting out and pushing it.

If you are in with a chance of winning, you have to be in contact with the leader at all stages – that means perhaps 20 yards in the early part of the race, 5 yards in the last few laps. Knowing what you do of your opponents, it is up to you to decide how far out you will start your finish, but your plan will have to be flexible, dependent on how you feel and how your opponents look. You have to beware of the 'multi-lap hypnotism' which seems to overcome runners in a large field. Runners frequently fall off the pace through nothing more than lack of faith in themselves. The laps tick by and they are still surrounded by other runners. They cease to believe that they can win, they start to feel tired, and they relax their concentration.

When somebody puts in a burst, you should immediately accelerate to his pace, so that the gap does not increase. Either he will be too strong for you and go away, or he will slow down and the gap will close. If in closing the gap you have drawn away from the men behind you, it may well be the right time for your own strike, while the man in front is still suffering. The long track races are more often decided by mental and physical strength than by tactics, but the principles given above should be applied to the the best of your ability. In a fast race, challenge late, but if the race is slow, it is often the man who has the courage to make the first decisive move who wins.

The steeplechase. If you are not used to steeplechasing, you will have to be particularly careful about running level pace, because the average pace per lap is much slower than for the corresponding flat distances. Seventy-two seconds a lap is a good speed for a female distance runner in a flat 3000m, but it is a very slow speed for a good male distance runner. However, this is the speed for a 9 minutes 3000m steeplechase, which is of a high standard. If you have international ambitions, you must be thinking of running each kilometre in 2 minutes 50 (68 seconds per 400m) for a time of 8 minutes 30.

Front-running is often an advantage here. First, you get a clear view of the obstacles (four wooden 3-foot barriers and a water-jump on each lap, for the uninitiated) and so can get your striding right and, second, it is much easier to break contact. If you go over a barrier first, you are into your running while the man behind you is still in mid-air; it is therefore easier to open a slight gap than in flat races. On the other hand, mistakes in pace judgement can be very costly indeed. The 1980 Olympics saw a classic race, where the Tanzanian, Filbert Bayi, led for almost the whole race, at world-record pace, only to be overhauled by the equally determined and more experienced Pole, Malinowski, on the last lap. It is an event which demands the utmost in physical and mental strength, because you have to keep on accelerating after each obstacle.

Middle distance team racing. In club, college, university

and international matches you are running as a member of a team rather than as an individual. Maximum points matter more than times. The coach or the captain should make sure that both runners have the same plan! Runners being the kind of people they are, they are often keener to beat the other member of their own team than the opposition. If the two team men are of equal ability, it must be agreed that roles will be changed from one match to another. If the opposition is either unknown or not very strong, then the team should set a fast level pace all the way, but with the best runner in second place at the bell so that he has time to collect himself for the sprint should that be necessary. If the opposition prove stronger than expected, the second member of the team should put in an all-out burst in the penultimate lap, with the number one just behind him. With luck, this will open a gap on the other team, so that when the number one makes his break, just after the bell, he will be well clear. If the second string runner is weak, the number one may have to do a lot of the leading in the early stages, but he should take a rest from doing *all* the work if the opposition is sitting on his shoulder.

Suppose you have two good men who both want to get a fast time. What is the fairest way of sharing the pace-making? If Runner A leads for the first 300m, Runner B takes over with three laps to go, and leads for one full lap and the next bend – that is, 500m. Runner A takes over again, and takes the pace for another 300m, when they reach the bell. In this way, although A is at a slight disadvantage, because B is sitting on him ready to attack, A has only been leading for the previous 300m and should be fairly fresh.

Long distance team racing. You will normally agree to take turns in leading. On the whole it is an advantage *not* to lead for the first few laps, so laps one and two may be slow, while each team tries to bluff the other into doing the work.

The team which decides to lead should do so decisively, with a sharp increase in pace, and they should obviously have agreed beforehand on who is going to do this. Once in the lead, the second man should stay close, so that he can move through quickly when he takes his turn in the lead. If the leader moves out and the second man comes through quickly on the inside, they will immediately open a gap on the rest of the field, and the man who now finds himself in second place should be aware of the gap. If he feels there is a chance of their breaking away he should tell the leader to speed it up.

In a 5000m, and certainly in a 10,000m, no one is going to break away in the first few laps. A furious early pace may frighten some weak runners, but it won't drop the good men, who will run at a slightly more even pace and stay fairly close. The team has to have a plan for when it will attack seriously, say with four or five laps to go, and when they *do* attack, the increase in pace should be dramatic.

Whatever the race, the last lap tactics are vital. If the field is closely bunched and your team is in the lead, the second man, who will normally be the best runner, should move up alongside the leader as they go into the top bend. This means that anyone trying a long finish has to run round both of you. As you reach the back straight, the number two man in the team should start giving it everything. The number one, if he is clever and confident, can let his second string get 3 or 4 metres ahead. If the opposition starts to overtake, he will naturally speed up, but otherwise, if it is still sitting on him, he will wait until after the 200m mark before putting in a really sharp burst and chasing his second string. He is thus giving his team the best possible chance of maximum points, even though he is gambling with his own chance of victory.

Mental preparation

If there's one thing about runners that impresses nonrunners, it is their mental strength. 'I wish I had your dedication,' they say; 'I don't know how you've got the will-power to go out every day,' or 'How do you keep it up, lap after lap? Don't you get bored?' In fact, there seems to be a general opinion that running is a question of mind over matter.

This, we know, is rubbish. All the positive thinking in the world won't change you from a 6-minute miler into a 5-minute miler – it's your training that does that, training which affects both body and mind. Your mental strength develops along with your physical strength – but of course you have got to have the will-power to get out and train in the first place.

Let's analyse the problems. There is the question of what running can do for you as a person. I am quite convinced that running has made me more positive, more confident, and more stable – not to mention healthier, more handsome and more modest! There are others who say that it is a dangerous addiction leading to obsessional neuroses and broken marriages. What I want to deal with here is the question of how to use your mind to get the best out of your body.

At least once a year, there comes for the competitive runner an occasion when he is staking everything – pride, status, physical condition, mental strength, the justification of his whole way of life. Success depends on beating other people, in the knowledge that they too are putting in everything they've got. You can't run like this every Saturday, but unless you are prepared to run like this sometimes you will never make the top. The reason for the saying 'Nice guys don't win' is that winning depends on a superabundance of naked aggression, applied in the right place at the right time. Many of us have the aggression surging within us like lava in a volcano, but the problem is to wall it in and channel it so that it delivers the necessary force at just the right time. This is where the right mental preparation comes in.

Pre-race preparation. This day has been fixed in your mind for weeks as the day on which you are going to produce your best. You have checked your training diary and seen that your training in the last two months has been better than this time last year. Sometime during the last week you have run a trial over one of your fixed distances to prove to yourself how well you are going. I like to run about half the race distance, or slightly less, on the Tuesday or Wednesday before the weekend race. During your two rest days you train gently, trying to go out at the same time of day as your race and rehearsing the events in your mind. You visualize yourself settling in calmly, cruising along inexorably behind the leaders. When you strike, it is going to be a strong, sustained strike. If someone comes past you, you are going to strike again. You are going to refuse to be beaten.

On the day of the race, you have your best kit prepared in advance. You have allowed plenty of time for travelling, including possible hold-ups, so you arrive early and have time to look round the course and rehearse it in your mind once again. You change without rush, you go through your usual length of warm-up and then you stay physically warm and loose, but mentally like a coiled spring, ready for the gun.

Techniques of mental preparation. Before I won the European 5000m, I had a litle mantra I used to repeat to myself while training. It went: 'Bruce is going to win, Bruce is going to win, who is going to win? Bruce is going to win.' It sounds trite, but it was the outward symbol of my motivation. Intellectually I had weighed up the opposition and reckoned that I had a good chance and I made my race plans. More importantly, on a basic emotional level, I had implanted the idea that I was going to win, whatever anyone else did. Winning my heat reinforced the conviction. When I came to make my burst, with 700m to go, it was as if something sprang out of my head and drew my body forwards, tired though it felt, over the last 200m.

This kind of training is known as 'autogenic' – that is, self-generated, positive mental training. It was originated fifty years ago in Germany by a Herr Schulz and is used extensively by the East Germans and other eastern bloc countries. The techniques are simple but definite. It can be regarded as a form of self-hypnosis. It both relaxes the body and strengthens the will; the result is the effect which I got through the repetition of my mantra.

Transcendental meditation may be calming, but I don't see that it can help you win, because it is non-directional. Many Christian athletes pray for the strength to win, and this may give them the vital inner conviction.

The role of the coach here is paramount. Most athletes need someone else to tell them that they are going to win, because they won't believe it themselves. The value of the great coaches such as Arthur Lydiard lies not in their knowledge, but the strength of their inner convictions which makes their athletes believe in themselves. The coach cannot hedge his bets. When it really matters he must commit himself to victory as unreservedly as the man running the race.

How to lose races. Even the novice runner has some sort of plan, though he probably won't stick to it. The experienced runner will have his ideal plan, but he will have to prepare himself for different eventualities, because all his main contenders will have *their* plans too. A common reason for failure, or under-performance, is that an opponent makes a move for which you are unprepared. This might not matter in chess, where you have half an hour for the next move, but in middle distance running a half-second delay is disastrous. The problem lies in applying your plan, or changing it, in the conditions of tremendous physical and mental pressure which apply. This is where race experience is essential.

Why athletes fail. 1. The wrong plan. When Jim Peters ran the Helsinki marathon he started much too fast, having a lead of 41 seconds at 5km. The fast start, coupled with the effects of a bad flight, meant that he was bound to slow. Once the front-runner has been caught and passed, *he never comes back.*

2. Lack of concentration. This is what happened to Sebastian Coe in the 800m in Moscow. He knew what he ought to do, but through lack of racing experience, he failed to concentrate on what was happening at the front. Just the reverse happened in the 1500m, where his intense concentration was clear to see and his immediate response to Straub's break was model tactics.

3. Lack of confidence. In every hard run there comes a time when your body says that it can't go on. Your experience tells you that you still have something left, and your motivation drives you on. If someone challenges you at that moment, it is a battle of personalities. The supremely confident or the highly motivated person will go on driving himself until the other person gives up or he himself collapses.

The classic race in which Roy Fowler beat Gaston Roelants for the international cross-country title in 1965 was a triumph of personality for Roy. He had few natural talents, but he made the best of those he had – an ability to train very hard and a willingness to fight to the bitter end. Gaston Roelants, himself a confident front-runner, just found it too tough in the long finishing straight and cracked completely. Front runners such as Dave Bedford and Ron Clarke have lost races in this way, because they were used to breaking away early on. In a race against men of near-equal ability, the first half of the race is a mere preliminary, and the front-runners cannot expect to break away until the end. Kuts managed to find that extra push in the twentieth lap, against Pirie in Melbourne in 1956, but Bedford in Munich, like Clarke in Tokyo, Kingston and Edinburgh, just could not find it.

12
The Runner's Life-style

Running should enrich your life, not diminish it. At the same time your life-style should help your running, not hinder it. The ideal situation is when your running blends with the other aspects of your life. If there is a clash of interests, something or someone is going to suffer.

By this stage, I hope that running will be an integral part of your personality. You should not feel the need to explain or apologize. Others around you will learn to accept that you are a runner and that running is a necessary part of your life. The best thing about the running boom is that we are now regarded as almost normal people rather than as freaks, and it is realized that running, though it may be an addiction, attracts a much better class of addict.

Health

If you exercise regularly, you are going to be a healthier person, but you are not superhuman. You can still pick up infections, and if you get over-tired from training you are more susceptible. There is no easy line to follow; you have to be tough with yourself and yet you have to look after yourself. You have to be able to tolerate pain and discomfort and yet you have to learn to recognize the more serious warning signals. The following guidelines should help:

1 Increase the amount of training gradually. Don't jump from 20 miles a week to 80 miles a week

2 Aim for regularity in the pattern of working, training, eating and sleeping

3 If you are feeling tired for the third consecutive time you go out training, have an easy day, regardless of what the schedule says

4 A runner who has had a hard race or a very hard training session is very similar to someone who is ill. His temperature is high, his blood sugar is low, he is sweating and he is dehydrated. He will be losing heat very rapidly, and so as soon as he cools down he should put on a track suit to prevent further heat loss. Rest, plenty of liquid and some easily digested food will restore him to normal health very quickly, within an hour or so, but if the runner does not look after himself he may take a couple of days to get back to normal.

5 If you have a slight cough or cold, you can usually go out training, as long as you keep warm. If you have a heavy cold, or influenza, so that you are feeling either very hot or slightly dizzy, you should *not* go training at all – it could be dangerous. If your pulse at rest and/or your temperature are well above normal, you should not go out training. If you have been ill, don't start running again until you have medical clearance.

Sleep. If a normal person can get along on eight hours a night, I would suggest that a runner needs an extra hour's sleep for every 10 miles run. The runner's worst problem is not sleeping the night before a race. I have found that it doesn't really affect your running, so long as you have the necessary eight or nine hours horizontal and as long as you don't *worry* about not having enough sleep. If you are changing time zones, try to adapt to the new time as quickly as possible by having a short run and a warm shower before going to bed. This will relax you. It is best to force yourself to switch to the new time immediately you arrive, and go training at the time dictated by the new zone. You may need as long as a day for every hour of the time change, before you are fully adjusted.

Diet. More nonsense is talked about this than any other aspect of running. If you look at a world championship line-up, you will see that it contains Mexicans living on beans and tortillas, Australians living on steaks, Californians living on junk food and Japanese living on rice and raw fish. Their diets are widely different, but the differences between the athletes' performances are measured in fractions of one per cent. There is no 'magic food' which will make you run faster – and world-class athletes do not rely on special foods. At most, they might take multivitamin pills, to ensure against a deficiency.

The human being is an omnivore. His digestive system breaks down the food into the raw materials and the cells take the things which they need. Most of these things are present in a balanced diet. If you are only running 3 or 4 miles a day, you will not need to eat any more than the non-runner, because most people eat more than they need anyway. If you are running 7 miles a day, you are burning up at least 700 extra calories a day. This is about twenty-five per cent of your normal daily energy consumption, since the average man consumes about 3000 calories a day; the average woman, who is of course considerably lighter, 2100 to 2500. The runner will feel more hungry as he runs more, and will unconsciously eat a bit more at each meal. The right way to take in this extra energy food is in the form of complex foods, e.g., bread, potatoes, or milk, because this will also increase his intake of proteins and minerals and vitamins. If he just eats chocolate he will get the extra calories, but nothing else. We do not know precisely whether athletes really need extra doses of minerals and vitamins when they are training hard, but if your all-round intake is increased by the necessary twenty-five per cent or more, along with your calorie intake, you will certainly not suffer from a deficiency.

The same argument applies to protein. Obviously we will tend to need more protein when we are working hard physically, because muscles are being built up, but the extra amount is probably covered by our normal diet. The recommended daily requirement of protein is 90 grams (3 ounces) for a very active person, and this protein may be obtained from animal sources (meat, fish, eggs, cheese) or from vegetable sources (bread, beans, lentils, nuts). Vegetarians who eat cheese, milk and eggs as well as vegetable products can satisfy all their dietary needs, and there are some very good vegetarian runners. Vegans, however, who eat no animal products, run the risk of going short of vitamin B12, and possibly calcium, iron and vitamin D as well. They are recommended to take yeast tablets to keep up their level of B-group vitamins, and to get as wide a variety of nuts, grains and vegetables as possible.

To sum up advice on diet, here are some guidelines:

1 Eat at least three times a day

2 Each main meal should include a protein source, an energy food and either fruit or green vegetables

3 The vitamin content of fruits and vegetables is higher when they are raw

4 Milk is recommended as a way of supplementing your diet if you are still hungry, as it is a well balanced food

5 In the energy foods, the complex ones, such as bread or pasta, are better for you than sweets or chocolate, because they release sugars into the bloodstream gradually, as they are digested.

Eating and racing. If you run soon after you have eaten, some of your blood supply has been diverted to your stomach, so you cannot function as well as usual. Furthermore, when your abdominal muscles contract, stitch, indigestion or vomiting may occur. The last meal before a race should be something easily digestible, mostly starch and protein, and it should be taken three or four hours before a distance race. If you are merely running slowly, however, food in the stomach will not bother you very much.

Eating glucose before a race will not make you run

better, and it may even have the opposite effect, a temporary rise in blood glucose may trigger off insulin production, and as a result sugar will be removed from the blood and stored in the liver. In long races (over the 1½ hour range) you may start to run down your carbohydrate reserve, and so drinking a dilute glucose solution in small amounts will help you. A strong solution may upset your stomach.

The marathon diet. The so-called 'bleed-out diet' can prove very useful to the low-mileage marathon runner. The high mileage runner (75 miles a week or more) is often doing long runs and depleting his store of glycogen, so his body builds up stores of it again. If he runs 15 to 20 miles five or six days before the race, and then continues to eat in his normal hearty way, he will build up a good store of glycogen while he is resting up. The low-mileage runner has to deplete himself by following the special plan. If he is running in a race on the Sunday, he should put in a long run, over 15 miles, on the Tuesday, and then deny himself carbohydrates for the next forty-eight hours. This means cutting out all sugar, bread, potatoes and other starchy foods, and eating mostly meat and vegetables, butter and cheese. He will feel pretty terrible by the Thursday afternoon, but from Thursday evening onwards he can eat plenty of carbohydrate.

All runners should beware of overdoing the carbohydrate or 'pasta-loading' binge on the night before a marathon race, because it can leave you feeling very bloated the next day. If you have followed the diet correctly, you may feel a little heavy in the first few miles, but you should feel much better than usual after 20 miles, if you are running at your usual pace early on.

Drinking. Drinking alcohol is not fatal for training, because it is metabolized by the body and used as a fuel. As long as the liver can break it down, and as long as the level in the blood does not build up, it will have no cumulative effects. I knew a European champion who drank two bottles of wine a day when in the training camp, but he was also running nearly 30 miles day. Beer can actually be good for distance runners, because it maintains their fluid balance and restores electrolytes – ions such as sodium, potassium and chloride. A lot of world-class runners have a drink and relax after their races, and it does them more good than harm.

In cool weather, extra fluid is just extra weight to carry, and you might even run faster if slightly dehydrated. In hot weather, however, it is essential to keep up your fluid level to avoid heating up, so it is a good thing to take in small amounts of water right up to the start of the race and to drink during the race. Do not wait for the symptoms of thirst, but keep 'topping up' by gulping a little water at each water station. It is not a good idea to take electrolyte drinks or salt tablets during the run, because that may cause vomiting, and if the solution is too strong it may cause water to be withdrawn from the blood, which is not what you want.

Smoking. Inhaling tobacco smoke has a damaging effect on the cells lining the bronchial tubes, and the tar from cigarettes can clog up the alveoli in your lungs. The occasional smoke, once or twice a week, will have no perceptible effect, but the more you smoke, the worse you will run. Sprinters can get away with it, because oxygen intake does not affect their performance.

Running and stress. Stress gets at us all sooner or later. Running enables you to handle stress better. For one thing, the chief effect of stress is the release of adrenalin, which causes an increase in heart rate and in blood pressure. If you go out and run it off, the blood capillaries open up and your blood pressure drops. Psychologically, running helps us to handle stress because we get used to increasing doses of stress in training, and by coping with this we become more confident in our ability to handle tough situations.

In times of worry and stress, we know that it helps a lot just to go out and run, preferably in tranquil surroundings. What you should not do is add to the stress by trying to fulfil training schedules to the letter, when you are already tired and over-loaded. That is using running in the wrong way. The stresses of work, moving away from home, emotional problems all add up to a total stress load, and if you add to that by trying to achieve training targets you will just get run down and depressed. In such a situation, go out and run easily for at least half an hour, without putting pressure on yourself.

Running and personal relationships

The runner is bound to be a self-centred person, but there is nothing wrong with that. Getting yourself into the right physical and mental state is necessary before you can deal with other people's problems. Too often, however, runners become so obsessive that they get things out of perspective. Running is supposed to make you a better all-round person, and there are times when missing a training session matters far less than looking after someone close to you. If you are putting in the last time-trial before going to the Olympics, it may take priority, but most of the time you can and should adjust your training in order to find time for other people.

The year-round strategy

At some time of the year – maybe summer holidays, maybe New Year – you are going to review your past year's running and decide on goals for the following year. This is where your training diary comes in. You should try to be as objective as possible and decide which were your most successful races and which were the ones you enjoyed most.

The next step is to decide which are going to be your most important targets for next year. Having decided that, you should analyse your past performances and decide what your weak points are, so that you have some sense of purpose in your training. Knowing what you are going for and what you are trying to do is essential in planning each season of the year.

You don't have to train all the year round in order to run really well at certain times. If there are times when you are going to be away or just too busy to take part in races, or even to train properly, you can make this just a 'maintenance' period. Even if you can only get out for two or three 20-minute runs a week, you will maintain most of your fitness for a couple of months. If it goes on for too long you will have to watch your weight, and you will lose out on stamina, but you won't fall back very far unless this period extends over three months.

When you come back from a holiday or a maintenance session you will have to build up training gradually again, but you should be able to race at the end of four weeks of running. This may be the time when you will start to build up again for serious running. I find it stimulating to have slightly different goals at each time of the year. In the autumn the weather is usually best for running long distances, and one can build up from the end of the summer holidays to be fit enough for a big race at the end of October – this is New York Marathon time if you are really ambitious. The road races extend into November, after which the weather gets worse and I tend to 'hibernate', cutting down the miles, but putting in a longer run or a hard hill session when the weather permits. January and February are cross-country months for the British runner, and the road runner should try this – see Chapter 8. In March the time comes to go for either the road or the track. You cannot do both at once with success. If you just run for the fun of it, you can switch from long races to short races, using one as training for the other, but after the first year you won't make much progress without a plan of racing, culminating in one or two peak periods of the year when you are going to run the races which matter most.

Overdoing it. Everyone has to progress at his or her own pace. An easy run for one person is a maximum effort for another. If you are ambitious, you can continue to increase both the amount and the intensity of your running, but there will come a time when you reach the maximum your body can cope with. The chief symptom is sheer tiredness, but minor illnesses, coughs, colds and leg strains will also become more frequent. The way to avoid this happening is to have one week of lighter training in every month, so that your pattern might go 60 miles, 55, 65, 40, and then back to 60. Allow yourself a couple of weeks of just easy running at the end of a competitive season before you launch into the next phase, and at some time of the year, give yourself one or two weeks with no running at all. This gives your whole system a chance to recover from any strain you may have been putting on it.

Resting up. This is just as important within the weekly programme as it is from one season to another. I suggest you work on either a weekly or two-weekly budget. At the beginning of each period, you should be fresh and eager to run. If this is not the case, you need another day's rest. If you feel tired from the day before, don't try to run it out by running hard, just run easy until you feel good again. Likewise, you should resist the temptation to put in hard training the day after a really successful race. The euphoria generated by your success may hide your fatigue, and another hard day may be just too much.

Coping with failure. The mark of greatness is the number of failures you can overcome. By failure you learn about yourself. Look back at your diary, and see whether it was due to lack of preparation. Consider your pre-race preparation and your tactics – you should be able to find a reason there, or at least an excuse. If neither of these helps, maybe you were just expecting too much. Maybe your best years are still in front of you, or maybe you are running in the wrong event. I cannot think of any runner I have known whom I would call a failure, except for those who gave up when faced with a temporary set-back. As long as you are still running, you are ahead of most people.

Coping with success. Enjoy it. Don't miss the chance of savouring even the little successes. Avoid the arrogance which shrugs aside praise. If you do not appreciate winning an event, you devalue the efforts of those who finished behind you. This is the time, too, to appreciate the efforts of those officials and helpers who have spent many hours and many days in organizing your race. When the congratulations subside and the medals have been handed out, it is time for re-evaluation. Sometimes you can feel a real sense of anti-climax. You have dreamed of winning this title for months, and now you have won it and nothing has really changed. You are still the same person. Don't be too sure. By winning a title and becoming a champion you are a different person in the eyes of the world. You are a winner, with an aura of success about you. The ordinary runner will feel that he has less chance of beating you, and the better runner may start to worry about you.

Now is the time to raise your eyes to the next horizon. Have you really been training your hardest? Is there not more still to come? Why not go for a higher level? If you try, you may fail, but if you don't try, you may never forgive yourself.

The older runner

Five years ago the question I had to answer was: 'Is it too late to start?' The success of the new wave of runners has answered that one. The most cited example is that of the New Zealander, Jack Foster, who took it up in his late thirties, just to get fit, and was silver medallist in the Commonwealth Games at the age of forty-one. Our own Libby Pfeiffer, starting in her mid-thirties, has gone from jogging housewife to the British Marathon Squad. At a more modest level, there are scores of men whose running career only started around the time of the 1981 London Marathon, who have come down from a 4-hour marathon to a sub-3 hours time in a couple of years. Jack Foster is still pioneering, nine years after his silver medal, with a marathon in 2 hours 20 at the age of fifty, and Clive Davies, in America, ran 2 hours 42 at the age of sixty-five. These are exceptional people, putting more time and effort into it than most can afford or would wish, but they show that it can be done. If Clive Davies, at sixty-seven, is still going for a sub-2 hours 40 marathon, then a target of, say, 10 miles in the hour, or even 5 miles in 30 minutes, seems less unreasonable for the hopeful forty-year-old.

The question is not: 'Can I do it?', but 'How do I do it?' Very carefully. Forget about your macho image. It is plain stupid to buy a pair of shoes and rush straight out of the door as if you're eighteen. If you want to start absolutely from scratch, I have gone over all that ground in *The Complete Jogger*. With a little common sense you can nurse yourself carefully through the early stages until you are up to a programme of regular jogging. If you are over thirty-five, you need to be fairly cautious about launching straight into the Jogger-into-Runner schedule in Chapter 4.

What about medical check-ups? If you are over thirty-five and are not used to regular exercise, it is a sensible precaution, because the check-up will reveal any gross abnormality, and you will also get a second opinion about how fit you are. You don't necessarily have to accept that opinion. There is a well known definition of an alcoholic as 'A man who drinks more than his doctor', and the same subjectivity will apply to his estimate of fitness. Some of my best friends are doctors, and their opinions about fitness are as different as their personalities and their figures.

Seriously, a routine medical check-up will be some help, but not a lot. Your best guide is your own feeling when you start running harder; if you start to feel something which is more than normal discomfort, particularly chest pains, stop running and see your doctor.

If you are seriously overweight, you will probably be given a recommendation to diet and lose weight *before* you start running. If you don't do this, the strain on your knees and ankles will be too much. You cannot expect a system which is equipped to cope with the stresses and strains of a 170-pound body to put up with the stresses of 230 pounds.

Even when you have got past these initial problems, the older runner should not expect to transfer directly to schedules designed for younger runners. The rate of growth and repair slows down as you get older, so you have to allow longer for the training to take its effect. Whereas I recommend the young athletes to alternate hard days and easy days, and then move on to two hard, one easy, I would recommend the older runner to start with one hard day to two easy days. Eventually you can move up to the same kind of training, if you are good enough, but you have to increase more slowly. For example, if we take the Jogger-into-Runner schedule in Chapter 4, the older runner would run the same number of miles in a week, but only do two of the 'quality' sessions in a week, the other days being steady running. He could get the six 'quality' sessions done in three weeks instead of two, and then start the cycle again, running a bit faster.

There are advantages to getting older. You are more stable, more balanced, less easily upset by little ups and downs. You can see things in a greater perspective and realize that it is not next week's race which is important, so much as over-all fitness over the next year, or the next ten years. The other advantage is that as you get older you can compete in easier age groups. When the over-forty competition starts to get a bit tough you can look around for races with an over-forty-five category.

The older you get, the more trouble you have to take in maintaining flexibility. Thorough stretching and warming-up should become a daily routine. Devotees of yoga and ballet training remain supple into their seventies and beyond, and this should be our aim too.

There is no reason why anyone should stop running. The oldest man to complete a marathon so far is a ninety-six-year-old Greek, but the centenarian marathon runner cannot be too far away – what a thought! I hope that as more old people run, it will become more a matter of course and less of an occasion for an exhibition. The eighty-year-old runner is not a freak and should not be encouraged to behave like one. Johnny Kelley the older is a good example of ageing gracefully. He won the Boston Marathon before the war and after it, as well as taking numerous second places. In 1981 he ran in his fiftieth Boston, and he is still capable of jogging along in under 4 hours, but he doesn't make a big fuss about it. He stays fit, runs regularly and competes very seldom.

Probably the question which is asked by everybody 'What is a good time for someone of my age?' This is an almost impossible question to answer, because we do not know whether you mean 'good' compared to the average person, the average club runner, or the international runner. The average person, aged thirty, would be doing well to run a mile in 7 minutes, the average club runner can probably beat 5 minutes and the international runner beats 4 minutes. The best veteran runners (over forty-five) can run under 4 minutes 20 for a mile. At longer distances the gap between the best veterans and international class is even narrower. As I have mentioned, Jack Foster was Commonwealth Games silver medallist, with a 2 hours 12 seconds marathon, at the age of forty-one. Miruts Yifter and Carlos Lopes have been at the very top of world class in cross-country and 10,000m, at the age of thirty-seven/thirty-eight. Now that more money is coming into the sport, I expect to see the best track and road runners staying at the top past the age of forty.

Try as we may, time must take its toll. The medical estimate is a fall-off in muscular strength of one-half a per cent to one per cent per year, and this ties up with my estimates on the fall-off in running performances. For a 6 miles/10,000m time, I estimate one loses a minute every five years. Converting this to the marathon, it means a fall-off of less than a minute per year, which is very little compared to the effects of either weather conditions or training on one's time. For a miler, it means a fall-off of 10 seconds every five years. If you could run 4 minutes for a mile and 28 minutes for 10,000m, at the age of thirty, you are going to be running about 4 minutes 40 seconds for the mile and 32 minutes for 10,000m at the age of fifty.

The encouraging thing about taking up running late in life is that for a while you can run the clock backwards. The average unfit thirty-five-year-old would be doing well to run 6 miles in under 50 minutes, but five years later he could be running it under 35 minutes, and twenty years later he could still be in better physical condition than he had been at thirty-five.

Injuries

Avoiding injuries. I hope that by the time you have been through my schedules the general principles will have become clear – increasing the load gradually, getting enough rest, maintaining one's equilibrium. In addition to this, the following points should be borne in mind:

1 Avoid training on the road for more than two consecutive days, if possible

2 When training on the road, use good training shoes, and do not go on using shoes when they are worn down

3 If your muscles are stiff, due to speed training or

sheer fatigue, do not do any hard training until the stiffness has gone. Long slow jogging, on soft going, is advised

4 Always precede races and hard training sessions with at least 10 minutes of jogging and thorough loosening and stretching exercises

5 Always follow races and hard training with a shower or bath. After very long runs in cold weather, a good soak in a hot bath is advisable

6 If a particular joint or muscle is tender or slightly inflamed, treat it with cold water or an ice pack for 5 minutes, *before* having your shower.

Treatment of injuries. For inflammations, severe stiffness and pulled muscles, the accepted treatment is ice, compression, elevation.

In practical terms, this means keeping an ice pack or a packet of frozen peas in the freezer. Hold the pack firmly against the inflamed area for as long as possible, remove it, then reapply. The next step is to use a bandage or tubigrip to limit further swelling, and then to keep weight off the injured area for a few hours. If you do this properly, you should be able to walk on the injured limb the following day, maybe even jog, and be training gently two days later. Plain aspirin, taken half an hour before running, is a good and safe anti-inflammatory.

If this treatment does not work, see a doctor or physiotherapist immediately, and follow their advice. It is the long-term future which matters. It may be upsetting missing next week's race, but the rest of the season and the rest of your life matters much more. If you suffer from persistent leg injuries, there may be some underlying defect in your skeletal system. You should see a sports doctor and try to find out whether orthotic supports in your shoes would help.

You only have one body, so look after it!

Useful Addresses

Southern Counties AAA,
Francis House,
Francis Street,
LONDON SW1P 1DL

Midland Counties AAA,
Devonshire House,
High Street,
Deritend,
Birmingham, B12 0LP

Northern Counties AAA,
Studio 44,
Bluecoat Chambers,
School Lane,
Liverpool L1 3BX

Welsh AAA,
Dr W. A. L. Evans, Hon. Sec.,
Winterbourne,
Greenway Close,
Llandough,
Penarth,
South Glam. CF6 1LZ

Scottish AAA,
16 Royal Crescent,
Glasgow G3 7SL

Road Runners Club,
D. Turner, Hon. Sec.,
40 Rosedale Road,
Stoneleigh,
Epsom, Surrey KT17 1JH

British Marathon Runners Club,
T. Lewins, Hon. Sec.,
13 Albany Road,
Old Windsor,
Berks.

English Cross Country Union,
B. J. Wallman, Hon. Sec.,
7 Wolsey Way,
Cherry Hinton,
Cambridge CB1 3JQ

Records

Men

Event	British	European	Commonwealth	World
800m	1:41.73	1:41.73	1:41.73	1:41.73
	Seb Coe 1981	Seb Coe 1981	Seb Coe 1981	Seb Coe 1981
1500m	3:30.77	3:30.77	3:30.77	3:30.77
	Steve Ovett 1980	Steve Ovett 1980	Steve Ovett 1980	Steve Ovett 1983
Mile	3:47.33	3:47.33	3:47.33	3:47.33
	Seb Coe 1981	Seb Coe 1981	Seb Coe 1981	Seb Coe 1981
3000m	7:32.79	7:32.79	7:32.10	7:32.10
	Dave Moorcroft 1982	Dave Moorcroft 1982	H. Rono (Ken) 1978	H. Rono (Ken) 1978
3000m	8:15.16	8:08.02	8:05.4	8:05.4
Steeplechase	Graeme Fell 1983	A. Garderud (Swe) 1976	H. Rono (Ken) 1978	H. Rono (Ken) 1978
5000m	13:00.41	13:00.41	13:00.41	13:00.41
	Dave Moorcroft 1982	Dave Moorcroft 1982	Dave Moorcroft 1982	Dave Moorcroft 1982
10,000m	27:30.3	27:22.95	27:22.4	27:22.4
	Brendan Foster 1978	F. Mamede (Por) 1982	H. Rono (Ken) 1978	H. Rono (Ken) 1978
Marathon	2:09:12	2:09:01	2:08:18	2:08:13
	Ian Thompson 1974	G. Nijboer (Neth) 1980	R. de Castella (Aus) 1981	A. Salazar (USA) 1981

Women

Event	British	European	Commonwealth	World
800m	1:59.05	1:53.28	1:59.0	1:53.28
	Christina Boxer 1979	J. Kratochvilova (Cze) 1983	C. Rendina (Aus) 1976	J. Kratochvilova (Cze) 1983
1500m	4:01.53	3:52.47	4:01.53	3:52.47
	Christine Benning 1979	T. Kazankina (USSR) 1980	Christine Benning 1979	T. Kazankina (USSR) 1980
3000m	8:37.7	8:26.78	8:37.7	8:26.78
	Wendy Sly 1983	S. Ulmasova (USSR) 1982	Wendy Sly 1983	S. Ulmasova (USSR) 1983
5000m	15:14.5	15:14.5	15:13.22	15:08.26
	Paula Fudge 1981	Paula Fudge 1981	Anne Audain (NZ) 1981	M. Decker (USA) 1982
10,000m	32:57.2	31:35.01	32:57.17	31:35.01
	Kath Binns 1980	L. Baranova (USSR) 1983	Ka Kath Binns	L. Baranova (USSR) 1983
Marathon	2:29:43	2:45:29	2:25:29	2:22:43
	Joyce Smith 1982	G. Waitz (Nor) 1983	A. Roe (NZ) 1981	J. Benoit (USA) 1983

Index